THE QUILTER'S GUIDE TO

ROTARY CUTTING

Other Books in the Contemporary Quilting Series

Fast Patch: A Treasury of Strip-Quilt Projects, by Anita Hallock

Fourteen Easy Baby Quilts, by Margaret Dittman

The Quilter's Guide to Rotary Cutting, by Donna Poster

Scrap Quilts Using Fast Patch, by Anita Hallock

Speed-Cut Quilts, by Donna Poster

Books in the Creative Machine Arts Series

Claire Shaeffer's Fabric Sewing Guide

The Complete Book of Machine Embroidery, by Robbie and Tony Fanning

Creative Nurseries Illustrated, by Debra Terry and Juli Plooster

Creative Serging Illustrated, by Pati Palmer, Gail Brown, and Sue Green

Distinctive Serger Gifts and Crafts, by Naomi Baker and Tammy Young

The Fabric Lover's Scrapbook, by Margaret Dittman

Friendship Quilts by Hand and Machine, by Carolyn Vosburg Hall

Innovative Serging, by Gail Brown and Tammy Young

Innovative Sewing, by Gail Brown and Tammy Young

Know Your Bernina, 2nd ed., by Jackie Dodson

Know Your Brother, by Jackie Dodson with Jane Warnick

Know Your Elna, by Jackie Dodson with Carol Ahles

Know Your New Home, by Jackie Dodson with Judi Cull and Vicki Lyn Hastings

Know Your Pfaff, by Jackie Dodson with Audrey Griese

Know Your Sewing Machine, by Jackie Dodson

Know Your Simplicity, by Jackie Dodson with Jane Warnick

Know Your Singer, by Jackie Dodson

Know Your Viking, by Jackie Dodson with Jan Saunders

Know Your White, by Jackie Dodson with Jan Saunders

Owner's Guide to Sewing Machines, Sergers, and Knitting Machines, by Gale Grigg Hazen

Petite Pizzazz, by Barb Griffin

Sew, Serge, Press, by Jan Saunders

Sewing and Collecting Vintage Fashions, by Eileen MacIntosh

Simply Serge Any Fabric, by Naomi Baker and Tammy Young

THE QUILTER'S GUIDE TO

ROTARY CUTTING

DONNA POSTER

Chilton Book Company
Radnor, Pennsylvania

Parents can give their children two things,
    the one is roots and the other is wings.

With loving thanks to—
My father,
    L. Harry Kershner,
        for giving me roots
and my mother,
    Alma Sitler Kershner,
        for giving me wings

Published in Radnor, Pennsylvania 19089, by Chilton Book Company

Designed by Anthony Jacobson
Illustrations by the author and by Rosalyn Carson
Manufactured in the United States of America

Library of Congress Cataloging in Publication Data
Poster, Donna.
   The quilter's guide to rotary cutting / Donna Poster.
     p. cm. — (Contemporary quilting series)
   Includes bibliographical references and index.
   ISBN 0-8019-8185-9 (hard) : ISBN 0-8019-8130-1 (pbk.)
   1. Quilting. I. Title. II. Series
TT835.P66 1991
746.9′7—dc20
                         90-55879
                         CIP

1 2 3 4 5 6 7 8 9 0   9 8 7 6 5 4 3 2 1

CONTENTS

FOREWORD

Even though the rotary cutter has revolutionized sewing and quilting, I know an intelligent grown-up who has sewn for years and who is still afraid of using her cutter. She's undoubtedly the tip of the iceberg.

Enter Donna Poster, queen of the speed-cut quilt. Donna's first book, Speed-Cut Quilts *(Chilton, 1989), showed how to use a rotary cutter and plastic templates to speed-cut 1,200 quilt blocks. Best of all, she organized us with a step-by-step Play-Plan: no more bare beds because of inertia. In that first book, she used her tools to cut specific blocks, like making Christmas cookies with bell-, tree-, and wreath-shaped cutters.*

But Donna has a what-if mind. What if I did this and this and this with the templates and the cutter? Couldn't I cut any shape?

The results are her second book, a broader guide than her first. Now you can make any shape of cookie cutter. The key is to determine the needed width, cut lots of strips, then chop shapes out of them. To help you practice, Donna has included instructions and templates for 20 quilts. With her usual thoroughness, she's figured yardages for seven sizes and offered alternate designs.

My friend with rotary cutter phobia, however, needs a house call. Since Donna runs a quilt shop, teaches, and travels, I doubt she'll stop by. But you could. Look outside your circle of fearless sewers and quilters. Does someone on the iceberg need help? Why not take your rotary cutter, template, mat, and this book to that someone's home for a few hours?

Robbie Fanning
Series Editor
Contemporary Quilting Series

Are you interested in a quarterly newsletter about creative uses of the sewing machine? For more information, write The Creative Machine, P.O. Box 2634, Menlo Park, CA 94026.

PREFACE

Hundreds of years ago, women made quilts by spinning the yarn and weaving the fabric. Only then could they begin to cut and sew.

Future generations bought their fabric at the store and their grandmothers said "Hmph! In my day we made our own fabric."

Then came the sewing machine. Those of our grandmothers who were fortunate enough to own one proudly used it to stitch their quilts. Their grandmothers said, "Hmph! In my day we pieced our quilts by hand."

Now we have the rotary cutter, and we're whipping out quilts like mad. And our grandmothers are saying, "Hmph! In my day we cut out each piece with scissors."

Following this progression I have a vision of one hundred years from now. Florabene is going to make a quilt. She hires a babysitter for little Cassiopeia (some things never change) and heads for the local quilt shop. There she selects her fabric and rents an hour on the quilting machine. This piece of equipment is about the size of a small room with hundreds of dials, buttons, and slots on the front. Florabene selects her quilt pattern, colors, and dimensions, then carefully feeds her fabric into the chosen slots. With all systems ready, she now pushes a central button that acti-

vates the machine. Buttons light up, dials turn, things go buzz, whiz and cachunk, cachunk!

Forty-five minutes later, with one huge belch, this machine spits out a gorgeous, finished quilt.

And our children, now grown up and grandmothers themselves, will undoubtedly say, "Hmph! In my day, we speed-cut quilts with rotary cutters. . . ."

ACKNOWLEDGMENTS

I am blessed in my classes with the greatest students. Those who took the classes for the twenty quilts in this book all knew that they were "guinea pigs" (their words, not mine).

Some were longtime quilters, and some had barely learned how to use the cutter. They all happily made suggestions and pointed out glitches here and there.

All of us laughed a lot the night we couldn't make anything work (and I knew it worked because I'd made the sample), only to find out I'd drawn the diagrams in the instruction sheet backwards.

These delightful people have been a great help and joy to me and I thank them all.

Special thanks to:

❧ P & B Textiles, for their contribution of fabrics for the Flower Basket quilt.

❧ Lael Alpiger, Julie Beck, Sharon Chambers, Suzette Harris, Diana Hylton, Teresa Kline, Kathy Lang, Sandy Lawrence, Sue Miller, Helen Oelkrug, Margaret Parks, Trina Rehkemper, Susan Reisser, Sue Saiter, Carol Shaffer, Nancy Smith, Lillie Spencer, and Barbara Tulloch for their stitching, suggestions, and encouragement.

❧ Sue Saiter, for helping at Needle Arts, giving me time to finish this book, and typing.

❧ John Anglin, for photographing the quilts.

❧ Allison Dodge, for the loving care she gave this book.

❧ Robbie Fanning, for teaching me how to be an author.

❧ Zoë and Laura Pasternak, my daughters, for their encouragement and never-ending faith in me.

❧ Arn Poster, who, besides developing the templates that made all this possible, cooked meals, ran my store, walked the dog, and hugged me a lot so I could finish this book.

Having fun with our new quilts

INTRODUCTION

As a quiltmaker, teacher, and shop owner, I have been fascinated by the rotary cutter since the day I sliced up my first pile of fabric. It seemed to me, however, that we should be able to do more with such a wonderful tool than cut up strips and triangles.

After much experimentation, I finally developed a series of plastic diamond and hexagon templates and my husband, Arn, began Holiday Designs to produce them. As an engineer, however, he was hardly willing to stop there. He began developing a vast range of cutting templates, including several he was told couldn't be done.

I began using these templates in my sampler classes with much success and soon compiled these methods into my first book, *Speed-Cut Quilts.*

At this point, I was running a quilt shop, teaching classes, and writing a book, which left me little time for stitching. So every time I got antsy and simply *had* to get to the sewing machine, I'd look over these templates to see if there was anything I could use to get it cut out fast. I was amazed at how much I could do with them.

Eventually, I came to realize that almost every piece in almost every pieced quilt could be speed-cut. I was ecstatic.

For over a year now, I have been experimenting on quilts, fabric, and students to bring you this book. With it you can take almost any quilt book you already own, plus any you may buy in the future, and translate the quilts for speed-cutting.

To make the book a little more interesting I have included instructions for 20 quilts using my speed-cutting methods. Each quilt has all the yardages and cutting information for seven sizes, including a tablecloth/lap throw (the square or oblong size). I've also included with each several options, plus a drawing that includes the seven sizes so it can be copied and cut to the size being made. In this way you can view the full quilt and actually count the number of pieces needed. Copy the page several times and have great fun filling it in with a #2 pencil or a box of colored pencils.

Some of these quilts are familiar old favorites, some are hard-to-find patterns of old favorites, and some are brand new. I've tried, whenever possible, to be authentic in naming these quilts, but many of the patterns came to me in the same way that quilt patterns, over the years, have always been passed around. So you may know some of these by a different name.

I've included a section on basic construction techniques. These are the ones I've found in my classes to work best for the most people. I feel strongly, however, that quilters must read, listen, experiment, and learn as many hints, techniques, and variations as possible. Gather up a neverending fund of knowledge, then choose whatever works best for you. Students in my beginning classes all hear my "ten quilters" story. I tell them if there are ten quilters in the same room, all doing the same thing, they are doing it ten different ways. And they are all correct!

So here's my newest book, I've had a wonderful time writing it—I hope you have a wonderful time using it!

Donna

1

SPEED-CUTTING EQUIPMENT

The recent development in tools has given today's quilter many more delightful options than her grandmother had. No longer do we have to spend days drawing and cutting around each separate piece for the quilt.

The secret to this new method of cutting is to get good equipment and to learn to use it effectively. With the rotary cutter and my Speedy System you can turn almost any pieced quilt pattern into a speed-cut project.

The time you'll save will astonish you. The first time I needed 792 odd-shaped pieces for a queen-sized quilt top, I timed myself. It took 1 hour and 15 minutes, and the pieces were so accurate that the sewing was a breeze.

The system I've developed involves the use of generic templates, taped, to define the pattern piece being cut.

There are dozens of templates currently on the market which are used for specific quilts. I have included several of these in the book plus alternative uses for them. For example, the template for the Double Wedding Ring makes a fine petal for the Little Dahlia (Chapter 3, Shape 17).

You'll find many advantages to my system. For the first time, hand piecers can enjoy the speedy methods, too. Instead of cutting across seams on pieced strips, you quickly cut stacks of pieces which can easily be hand pieced.

Specialized fabrics that would be difficult to draw shapes on, such as lamé, are a cinch to cut with the rotary cutter.

Specific placement of fabric designs is easy with the see-through acrylic templates.

Mirror-image patterns are cut by simply flipping the template over or by stacking all layers with like sides together.

Teresa and Helen planning a quilt

The accuracy in cutting is nothing short of a stitcher's dream. Imagine cutting twelve layers of fabric even with the finest of scissors: It would be almost impossible to cut the top and bottom layers the same. With the rotary cutter, they are identical. Cut edges are straight, even, and precise, making the stitching a snap.

These time-saving tools make piecing much easier and more enjoyable. Our goal, of course, is to have a lovely quilt when finished, but how much nicer it is when we've also enjoyed the process of making it.

Choosing Your Equipment

Anyone who has shopped for cereal lately knows the confusion of choosing one brand. The world of the rotary cutter is no less confusing to the novice.

As with all equipment, there are pros and cons for all the types available. What appeals to Sally may be objectionable to Nancy.

I hope the following comments will help you decide which equipment to purchase. They are based on observations made by my students over the many years I've been teaching classes using the rotary cutter.

In this chapter, I will discuss basic equipment (rotary cutter, cutting mat, and rotary cutting rulers and templates), helpful extras, and my recommended starter set. Other quilting equipment is described in Chapter 4.

Basic Equipment

Rotary cutter. This is a cutting tool, resembling a pizza cutter, with a very sharp, circular blade. Because the blade is so sharp, a guard is necessary.

All of the currently available cutters seem to be of good quality, sturdy, and easily adapted to right- or left-hand use. They all include high-quality blades. Replacement blades are readily available.

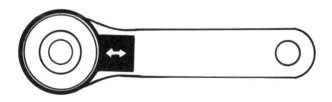

Some cutters are available in two sizes. For straight edges, the larger, heavy-duty cutter is easier to use, cuts faster, and gives you better control. Curves can be cut more easily with the smaller size.

The differences my students and I have noticed are:

Olfa: Features a guard that is easily clicked on. I teach my students to "push that thumb" at the end of *every* cut. After a very short time, this becomes an automatic movement.

Dritz and *Kai:* Arthritic people love these brands because the guard moves back automatically as you press down to cut. However, it is easily pushed back by small, inquisitive fingers, too.

But if you have no little children around, these are wonderful cutters.

Quilter's Rule: The shaped handle is easy to grasp and appeals to many people with arthritic or handicapped hands. The guard is not so easily clicked on and off, but an added safety feature is that it can be locked in place when not in use.

Cutting mat. I strongly recommend that you invest in a self-healing mat specifically made for use with the rotary cutter. Using any other type of surface will quickly dull the blade, and having to replace the blade constantly is costly and aggravating.

In purchasing a mat, look for these points:

1. *Size.* One side of any mat should be at least 23–24″ long to accommodate a folded piece of 45″ wide fabric. Narrow ones are great for toting to classes. For home use, treat yourself to the biggest one you can afford or have room to store. (My editor stores hers under the bed.)
2. *Finish.* A matte finish with a slightly rough feel will help keep your fabric from slipping. The slicker the surface, the more difficult to use.
3. *Grids.* Many mats are available with one-inch grids on one side—nice but not necessary. The narrow ones we use for class are plain, so my students learn all techniques without them.

My students tell me the Olfa mat must be stored flat and away from extreme heat. If not, it will warp. This seems to be compensated, though, by its surface, which gently helps control the fabric. The Kai mat is dark blue on one side and cream-colored on the other. This feature is most helpful for people who have difficulty distinguishing color or tones.

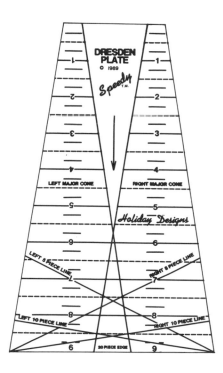

Rotary cutting rulers and templates. Here's where you enter a world of mass confusion. With dozens of rulers and templates on the market, how does a beginner pick and choose?

First, understand the difference between specialized templates and general-use templates. Specialized templates are used for only one shape. To make all the quilts you dream of, using only specialized templates would mean buying hundreds.

Instead, with my Speedy System, you can use a general-use template for many shapes. You merely tape different areas on the general-use template for cutting guidelines. For example,

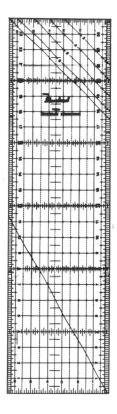

with my Speedy System, you can cut a hexagon with a 60° diamond template.

Even though I will give you many options for templates, many specialized templates simply cannot be substituted. In Chapter 3, I have included instructions for using only three of these (Double Wedding Ring, Drunkard's Path, Dresden Plate) for a second purpose. Learn to look at all specialized templates in this way.

I've set up some guidelines for you to follow, but you will eventually have your own favorite assortment of templates. Purchase a set with an eye to variety and ease of use.

Rulers and templates to be used with the rotary cutter are very different from those meant for other uses. You'll need to look for these points:

1. They should be made of sturdy, clear acrylic and be a bit over $1/16''$ in thickness.

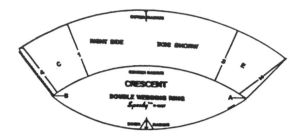

4. The length of your basic strip-cutting ruler should be 23–24″, long enough to span a folded piece of 45″-wide fabric. The ruler should be at least 6″ wide. Narrow rulers are more difficult to hold in place. My personal favorite is my husband's Miterite, as it is 8″ wide and cut at a 45° angle on one end, serving a wide variety of purposes.

2. The edges should be straight, not rounded, so the blade will ride smoothly against them.

3. The markings should be easy to read, with ¹/₈″ and ¹/₄″ markings easily distinguished from the 1″ markings and from each other.

5. The surfaces should be smooth enough to slide easily. This helps in accurately positioning the rulers and templates on the fabric.

Helpful Extras

¹/₄″ quilter's tape. Best tape to use on your templates. It is narrow and leaves little residue. Whenever possible, apply it to the *unprinted* side of your template. If you must use it on the printed side, use very small amounts and remove it as soon as possible.

WD 40 or Goo Gone. Excellent products for removing any tape residue.

Rotary cutter replacement blades. Always keep extra blades handy as they will get dull or nicked in time. Whenever I'm about to cut out a whole quilt—twelve layers at a time—I change blades. It's worth it for the time it saves and the resulting neatness. A hint on changing blades: As you remove the cutter parts, lay them down in the order you took them off. When you get to the blade, change it, and the parts are all lined up, ready to put back on. Safety Note: I put the old blade in the packaging from the new blade, then tape it heavily before I discard it.

Slide and grip strips. These grip the fabric when you press down on the template, keeping it firmly in place. Use small pieces, about ¹/₂″ square, sparingly, as you'll want to slide the template when positioning it. I place them ¹/₄″ in from all cutting edges, about 4–6″ apart. Put them on the top and bottom, so you can turn the template over if needed.

Handle. The handle attaches to the top side of the template, making it much easier to reposition for the next cut without mussing your pile of fabric. Also, the lines on your template will last much longer because you'll be lifting it more often rather than sliding it, which erases the lines. These handles are easily removed as needed.

Line savers. These are cut into small pieces (¹/₂″ square) and attached to the printed side only. They lift the template slightly above the fabric, preventing the lines from being worn off as quickly.

My Recommended Starter Set

Large cutter

9″ × 23″ mat

Spare blade

Ruler, for squaring corners and cutting strips, bias tape, 45°, 90°, 135° triangles, angles, and mitered borders. (I prefer my husband's Miterite.)

12¹/₂″ square for squaring corners and blocks, cutting squares and rectangles from ¹/₂″ to 12¹/₂″.

60° diamond, for cutting 30°, 60°, and 120° triangles and angles.

¹/₄″ quilter's tape

These pieces would set up a very basic rotary-cutting system. Add pieces, then, as you need them.

All of the supplies mentioned in this chapter are available in quilt shops. If you do not have access to a quilt shop, you can order them by mail from the Supply List at the end of the book.

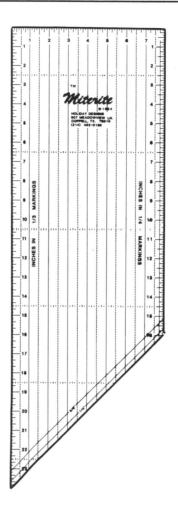

2

BASIC TECHNIQUES OF ROTARY CUTTING

Using the edge of a ruler or template as a guide, just roll the cutter blade through layers of fabric to cut it.

Yes, it really is as simple as that! But there are ways to make cutting even easier. Here's how:

🍃 *Handling the Fabric.* Fold the fabric as it was folded on the bolt, keeping the selvages even. If the layers do not lie smooth, do not force them. Just lift the top layer and move it gently to one side until it automatically lies flat. Position fabric on the cutting mat (Fig. 2-1). (A left-handed person will lay the fabric on the left side of the mat.) To cut multiple layers, stack them with the folds even and the selvages parallel. I cut as many as 12 layers. Practice first!

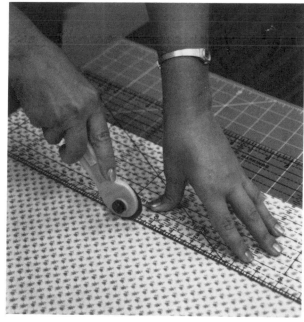

Using the rotary cutter

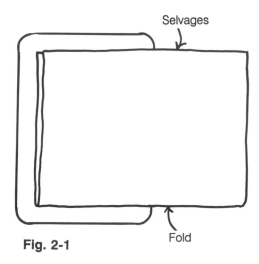

Selvages

Fold

Fig. 2-1

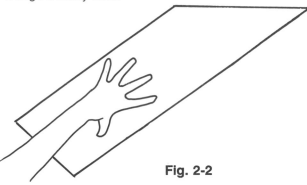

Fig. 2-2

🍃 *Handling the Ruler.* Holding your left hand like a tent, place your thumb and forefinger ½–1″ in from the cutting edge with remaining fingers in a comfortable position

(Fig. 2-2). Press *down* firmly. This prevents the ruler from moving and presses the layers of fabric firmly together. When cutting a 22″ span, press on one end of the ruler while cutting, then, carefully walking your hand to the other end, finish cutting.

🔹 *Handling the Cutter.* Pull the guard back to expose the blade. Hold the cutter at a comfortable angle, with the blade side next to the ruler (Fig. 2-3). The blade must be perpendicular to the ruler. If held at an angle away from the ruler, it will damage both the ruler and the blade (Fig. 2-4). As you cut, press the cutter *down* firmly and slightly against the ruler. Always cut away from you, as this gives you the best control. Be sure to flick the guard on at the end of *every* cut. Safety measures are extremely important. Treat the cutter with the same measures of caution that you use with kitchen knives and sewing shears.

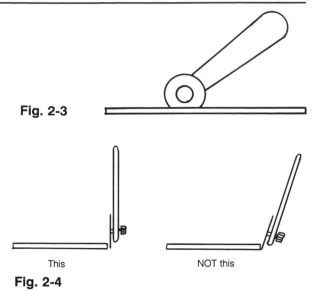

Fig. 2-3

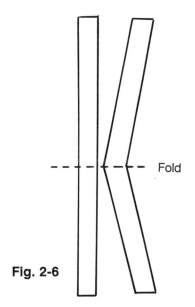

This NOT this

Fig. 2-4

Using the Ruler

The portion of ruler on the fabric will determine the size of the piece you'll cut. For example, if cutting a 2″ strip, place 2″ of the ruler on the fabric and let the rest of the ruler hang off (Fig. 2–5).

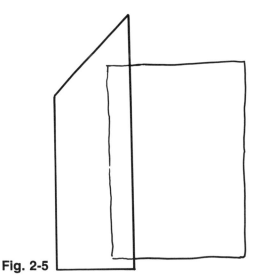

Fig. 2-5

That's my general rule of thumb for my whole Speedy System. Here are some other rules to follow:

🔹 The first cut on any piece is made to trim the raw edge of the fabric. This cut must be 90° to the fold. Otherwise, instead of the strips being straight, they will be angled (Fig. 2-6).

Fold

Fig. 2-6

There are several ways to do this. My favorite is to place the 1″ cross-mark of the ruler on the fold. The cutting edge is then at a 90° angle (Fig. 2-7). You'll need to move to the other side of the table to make this cut (*never* try to cut under your arm!).

A second method is to place a large square template on the fold to determine the 90° angle, then position the ruler against it (Fig. 2-8). Carefully remove the square and cut against the ruler. *Caution:* it is very easy to move the ruler out of position without realizing it.

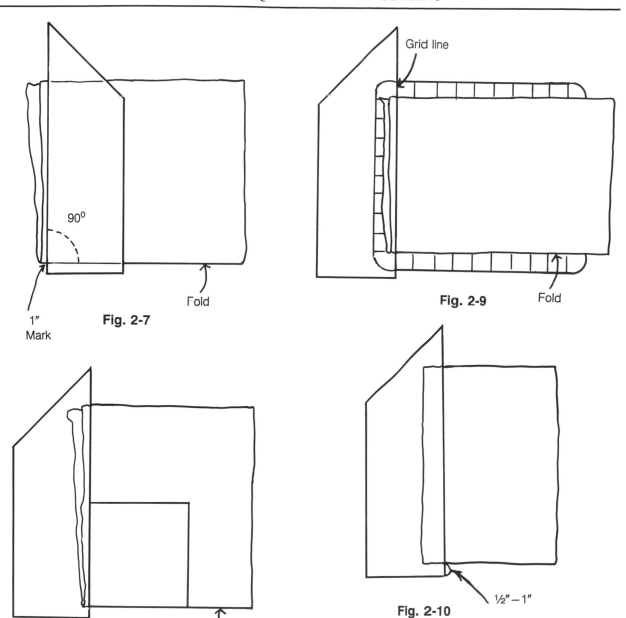

Fig. 2-7

90°

1″ Mark

Fold

Grid line

Fig. 2-9

Fold

Fig. 2-8

Fold

Fig. 2-10

½″ − 1″

A third method can be done only on a gridded mat. Place the fold on one of the horizontal lines and line up the ruler with a vertical line (Fig. 2-9). This is a fast and easy method, but you must be careful to keep the fold on that line. If your mat has a slick surface, use the first method.

❧ Always position the ruler ½″ or more below the starting point of a cut. Otherwise, you'll nick the corner of the ruler and very quickly ruin the blade (Fig. 2-10).

❧ When positioning a ruler or template, lean over the table and look straight down. Otherwise your cut will be wrong by the thickness of the ruler.

❧ Whenever possible, use the same ruler throughout a project as rulers are *not* exactly alike. With my Speedy System, however, this is not as important as it once was.

❧ I've tried cutting batting—it doesn't work! The blade just imbeds all those little white fibers into a never-to-be-healed slice in the mat.

Cutting Basic Strips—Beginner's Fun

Let's have some fun now! You've learned the basic cutting techniques, and it's time to try a few strips. Practice first! If you don't have any scraps of good quality fabric (poor fabric will behave badly and dull your blade), invest in a yard or two of good muslin. The practice time will be well worth it.

Step 1. Trim fabric (Fig. 2-7).

Step 2. Place the 3″ ruler marking on the trimmed edge (Fig. 2-11).

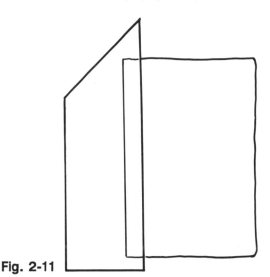

Fig. 2-11

Step 3. Cut!

You've done it! No fooling—that's all there is to cutting strips.

Now here are a few hints for cutting lots of strips:

  Put some ¹/₄″ masking tape on the ruler line you're using. It's too easy to whiz along, be distracted, and plunk that ruler on the wrong line. The tape will catch your attention. *Note:* Always put the tape *outside* the cutting line. The tape should never end up *on* the piece to be cut (Fig. 2-12). Tape on the *unprinted* side of the ruler whenever possible so you don't pull off the printing.

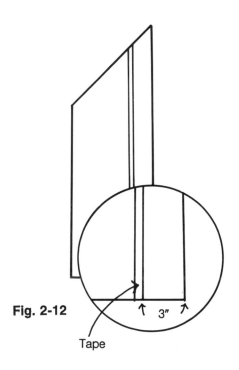

Fig. 2-12   ↑ 3″ ↑

Tape

  Every third or fourth strip, check the 90° angle. If it's off a bit, retrim the edge.

More Beginner's Fun

Just for fun, let's cut some squares from that strip you just made.

Step 1. Trim end of strip to 90° (Fig. 2-13).

Step 2. Place the 3″ ruler line on the trimmed edge (Fig. 2-14).

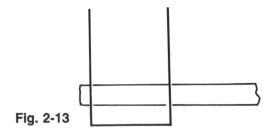

Fig. 2-13

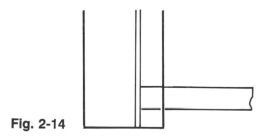

Fig. 2-14

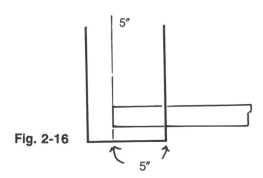

Fig. 2-16

Step 3. Cut.

Now is this fun or what? Do a few more. Just keep aligning the cut end of the fabric with the 3″ line of the ruler and cut (Fig. 2-15).

How about some triangles? Just place the ruler from corner to corner on one of the squares (Fig. 2-17). Cut!

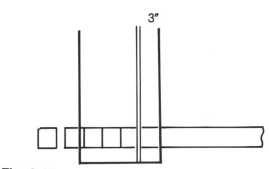

Fig. 2-15

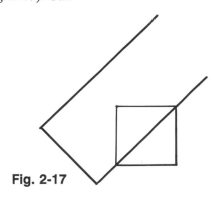

Fig. 2-17

Want a rectangle? Move the cut end to the 5″ ruler line (and move the tape) and cut (Fig. 2-16).

It's so easy! All you do is cut some strips, then chop your pieces out of that strip.

You've just opened the door to a whole new world. Now come along with me and I'll show you, one by one, how almost every quilt piece in any quilt can be cut like this!

Using the Basic Strips

Cutting strips is the basis of almost all rotary cutting. Following are some of the most common uses of these strips. Play with these a bit—they're fun. (Cut 2″ strips throughout.)

Cutting across Multiple Strips to Form Units

1. Sew two strips. Cut units same width (2″ here) as original strips (Fig. 2-18).
2. Turn alternate units 180°. Stitch together (Fig. 2-19).

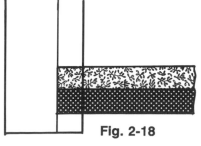

Fig. 2-18

Fig. 2-19

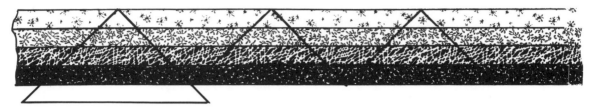

Fig. 2-20

Cutting Shapes from Units of Strips

1. Sew several strips. Cut triangles (Fig. 2-20).
2. Turn units. Stitch together (Fig. 2-21).

Fig. 2-21

Cutting Bias Strips

With the rotary cutter this method is faster than the "continuous bias tube method."

1. Trim end of fabric so it forms an exact 90° angle (Fig. 2-7).
2. Open to single thickness. Fold cut edge to meet selvage edge (Fig. 2-22).

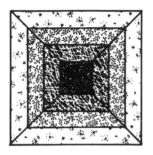

Selvage

Cut Edge

Selvage

Fig. 2-22

3. If length of diagonal fold is longer than ruler, fold upper point down to lower point (Fig. 2-23).

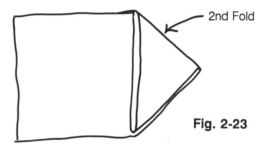

2nd Fold

Fig. 2-23

4. Remove diagonal folded edge by trimming ⅛″ from it (Fig. 2-24).

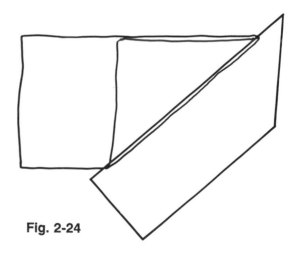

Fig. 2-24

5. Cut bias strips of desired width (Fig. 2-25).
6. Sew bias strips end to end, right sides together, with a ¼″ seam (Fig. 2-26).

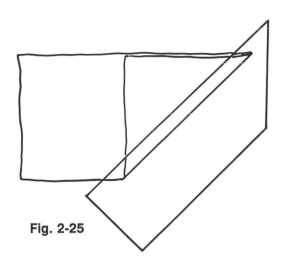

Fig. 2-25

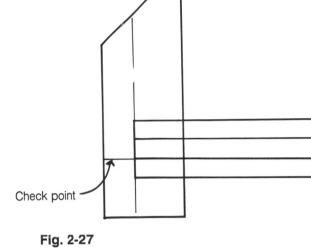

Check point

Fig. 2-27

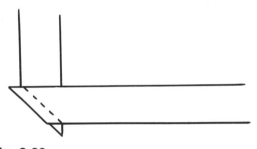

Fig. 2-26

Cutting Borders and Lattice Strips

1. If you don't mind seams showing periodically throughout the border, cut strips across the fabric and seam them to make one long strip. Then sew them to your quilt.
2. To make an unpieced border, cut strips along the length of your fabric. (Length of fabric must be at least as long as the border being cut.)

A Few Hints for Cutting

❧ When cutting across seams, check the 90° angle along a seam, *not* an edge. This is much more accurate. If your ruler has cross lines, use these as checkpoints by placing one on a seam with every cut (Fig. 2-27).

❧ To cut down on bulk, stagger seamed units by placing the cut edges parallel to the seams approximately 1/4" from each other. This will place the seams side by side instead of on top of each other (Fig. 2-28).

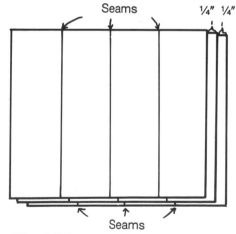

Seams   1/4" 1/4"

Seams

Fig. 2-28

❧ Occasionally, a pattern will require the strips to be cut lengthwise. To do this, open fabric to single thickness and fold selvages back and forth, accordion style (Fig. 2-29). Use first cut to trim selvages away (Fig. 2-30). Cut strips from this edge.

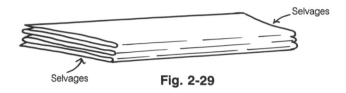

Fig. 2-29

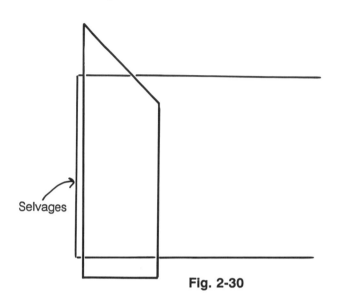

Selvages

Fig. 2-30

Method 2. If your mat has grids, line up the folded fabric with a horizontal line, making the first vertical cut at the "0" line on the grid. Place ruler on the grid marking for the border width you need and cut (Fig. 2-32).

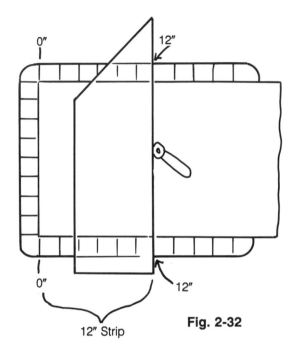

Fig. 2-32

12" Strip

🍃 There are several ways to cut borders wider than the width of the ruler.

Method 1. Determine the number of extra inches needed and place a square template over that amount. Position ruler next to it and cut (Fig. 2-31). *Caution:* Check "excess" measurement across entire width of fabric.

Method 3. Measure from cut edge and mark at two points. Place ruler on these marks. Cut (Fig. 2-33).

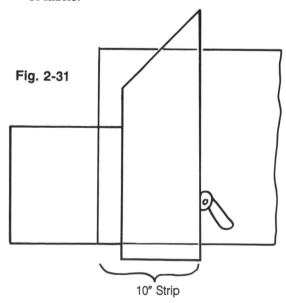

Fig. 2-31

10" Strip

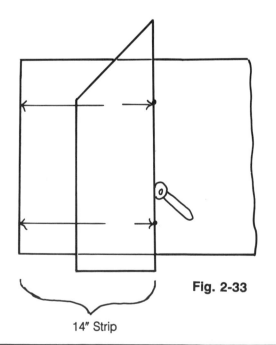

Fig. 2-33

14" Strip

ᐓ Large blocks can be cut the same way as wide borders. Cut strip the width of the block. If needed, carefully move this strip one-quarter turn on the mat. Cut block to desired length (Fig. 2-34).

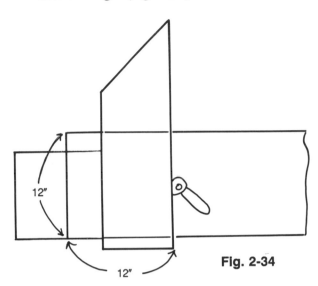

Fig. 2-34

ᐓ Dress pattern pieces can also be cut with the rotary cutter. Use weights instead of pins. Use a small cutter to manipulate the curves and a ruler for straight lines. It's easier to cut with the pattern to the left of the ruler when you can. And definitely treat yourself to a big mat for this and a tabletop you can move around, since you can't easily turn the fabric.

ᐓ Trimming odd and uneven edges from a quilt top is easy with the rotary cutter (Fig. 2-35).

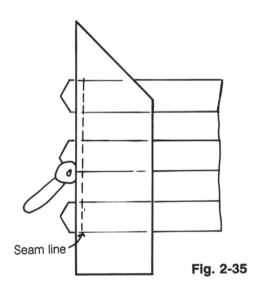

Seam line

Fig. 2-35

Donna's Speedy System

Now that you're an expert at cutting strips, let's move on to shaped pieces. My fast and easy Speedy System consists of simply cutting a stack of strips, then chopping stacks of quilt pieces out of these strips.

Here are the three basic steps:

Step 1. Find or create two parallel lines by simply placing your ruler on one edge and taping the parallel edge. Cut strips to this width (Fig. 2-36).

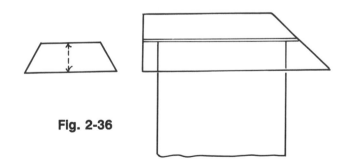

Fig. 2-36

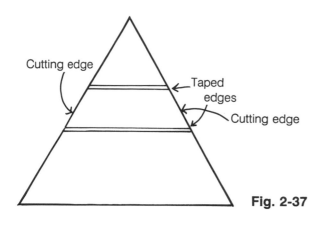

Cutting edge

Taped edges

Cutting edge

Fig. 2-37

Step 2. Place template over pattern piece. Tape as indicated. You now have:
A. Cutting edges
B. Taped edges—these will be used to match previously cut edges (Fig. 2-37).

Step 3. Use taped template to cut many pieces from stacked strips (Fig. 2-38).

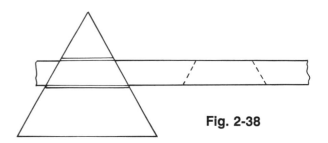

Fig. 2-38

Preparing to Cut

Using the Speed-Cutting System

Chapter 3 offers instruction on rotary-cutting 30 of the most used quilt pattern shapes and their variations. You will, by using and experimenting, quickly learn to recognize them for use in all your future quilts:

Each page contains the following information:

1. The basic shape of pattern piece (Fig. 2-39).

Fig. 2-39

2. Several variations of this piece (the variations are endless!) (Fig. 2-40).

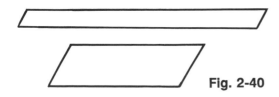

Fig. 2-40

3. Finding or creating the basic strip (Fig. 2-41).

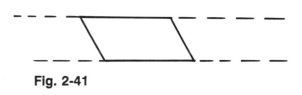

Fig. 2-41

4. Taping and using the basic template (Fig. 2-42).

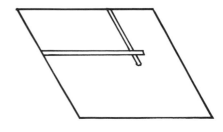

Cut from strip

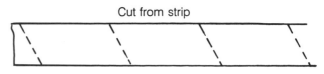

Fig. 2-42

5. Optional choices of templates (Fig. 2-43).

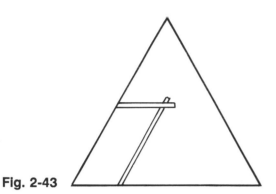

Fig. 2-43

Taping the Template

1. Choose a template or ruler to fit the shape of the design to be cut. Pattern must include seam allowances.
2. Place template on pattern, lining up two outer edges of tool with pattern. Tape all other pattern sides on tool with masking tape. Place tape *around* the pattern, not inside it. When laying tape down, lean over the table, so you are looking straight down on the pattern.
3. Instructions will refer to the "cutting edge" and the "taped edge" of your template. *All cuts are made on the cutting edges.*

Speedy System Specifics

🍃 The Speedy System instructions are for cutting multiples of a piece. To cut single units, tape template as usual, but instead of starting with a strip, simply cut, rotate, and cut again (Fig. 2-44).

🍃 Cutting circular edges is not quite as neat as straight edges. Use the smaller cutter and short, choppy strokes. This allows the layers to ease back in place.

🍃 At times you'll need to flip a template over or rotate it (Fig. 2-45). This will seem awkward at first, but with practice, will feel very natural.

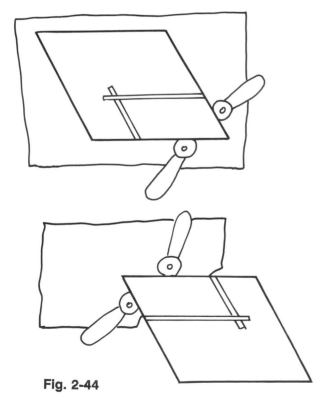

Fig. 2-44

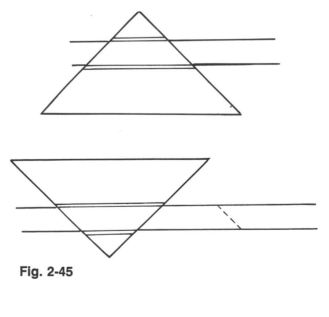

Fig. 2-45

❧ When cutting small portions from a stack of fabrics, prop the rest of the template on a stack of the same height (Fig. 2-46). Otherwise, your cuts may be inaccurate.

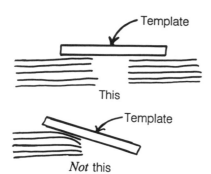

Fig. 2-46   *Not* this

❧ Most pattern pieces can be cut with no regard to layering. However, learn to recognize the following:

1. *"Like" pieces.* Patterns repeat in a "like" fashion (Fig. 2-47). The fabrics must *all* be stacked with *right* sides up.

Fig. 2-47

2. *"Mirror" pieces.* Patterns repeat in a mirror, or opposite, fashion (Fig. 2-48). The fabrics must be stacked with *like* sides together, in the same way as for cutting a garment.

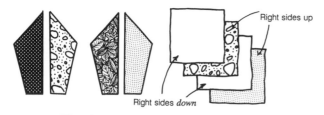

Fig. 2-48

❧ You will still occasionally use scissors. I think of the rotary cutter as the microwave of quilting, but when you own one of these, you still sometimes use the range and oven.

❧ A template to be used for a circle or arc for appliqué may be of a slightly different shape than the pattern piece. The unit will assume the correct shape when pressed around the pressing template (Fig. 2-49).

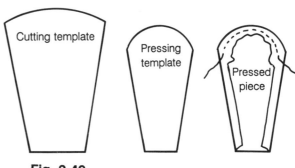

Fig. 2-49

❧ You may, at times, find a curved piece that simply does not match any cutting template. Cut a pattern from stiff plastic (available at fabric or quilt stores or by mail order—see Supply List at the end of the book). You can cut three or four layers of fabric with this and the small rotary cutter. You must, however, cut carefully as the blade will easily cut the plastic. Another option is to draw around this template and cut the three to four layers with scissors.

❧ Angles are often referred to in terms of degrees and it helps to recognize the shapes. Figure 2-50 shows the most common. A 60°/120° template is not interchangeable with a 45°/90° template.

❧ The ruler and templates pictured throughout this book are the Miterite and Speedies from Holiday Designs. Many others can be used. These are simply my personal favorites since they were designed for my Speedy System. Use whatever you're more comfortable with.

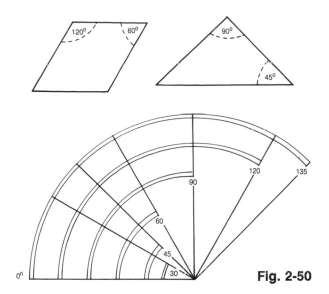

Fig. 2-50

Now that you've learned my Speedy System you can cut out any quilt in much less time and more accurately than before! You've really found a way to buy, for yourself, some extra time and pleasure.

3

30 BASIC SHAPES TO SPEED-CUT

Following are instructions for speed-cutting 30 shapes. Each shape is used in at least one of the 20 quilts featured later in this book.

For each of these 30 shapes, I name the template you will need (for example, square or 60° diamond). You will have many of these templates on hand. Others (as the Dresden Plate) can be found in the Templates section later in this book. I also name two specialized templates you may not be familiar with: The Miterite is an 8″ × 24″ ruler with one end cut off at a 45° angle. The 45° Master Speedy is a 7″ × 10″ rectangle with one corner cut off at a 135° angle. As you will see by studying the optional templates listed for each shape, these two basic templates can be used to cut the major portion of your quilt pieces.

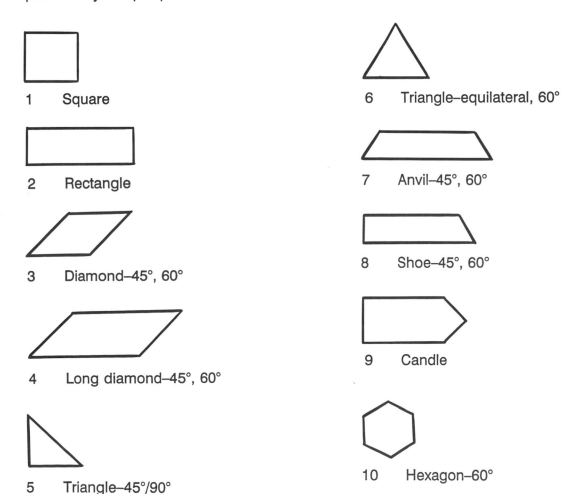

1   Square

2   Rectangle

3   Diamond–45°, 60°

4   Long diamond–45°, 60°

5   Triangle–45°/90°

6   Triangle–equilateral, 60°

7   Anvil–45°, 60°

8   Shoe–45°, 60°

9   Candle

10   Hexagon–60°

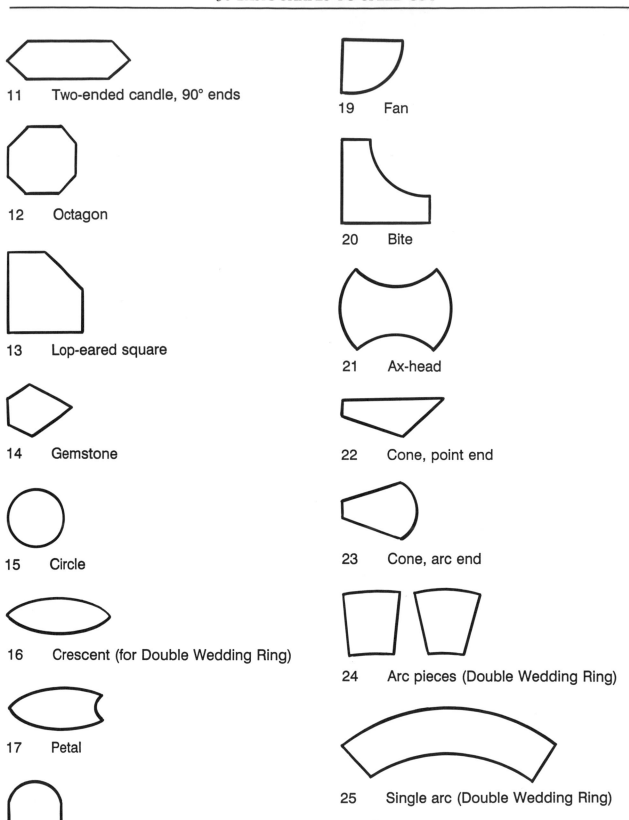

11   Two-ended candle, 90° ends

12   Octagon

13   Lop-eared square

14   Gemstone

15   Circle

16   Crescent (for Double Wedding Ring)

17   Petal

18   Archway (for Clamshell)

19   Fan

20   Bite

21   Ax-head

22   Cone, point end

23   Cone, arc end

24   Arc pieces (Double Wedding Ring)

25   Single arc (Double Wedding Ring)

26   Odd-shaped triangle with a 90° angle

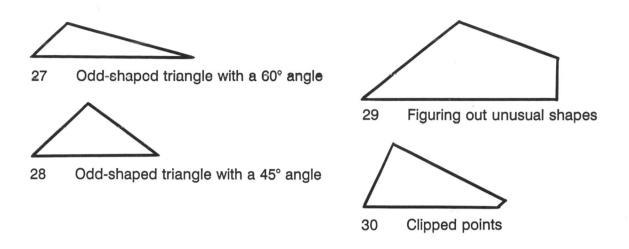

27   Odd-shaped triangle with a 60° angle

28   Odd-shaped triangle with a 45° angle

29   Figuring out unusual shapes

30   Clipped points

1. Square

Basic Shape   ## Variations

Basic Strip   ## Taping and Using Basic Template (Square)

Cut from strip

Optional Templates

90° corner
   45/90° triangle
   Basic ruler
   45° Master
   Miterite

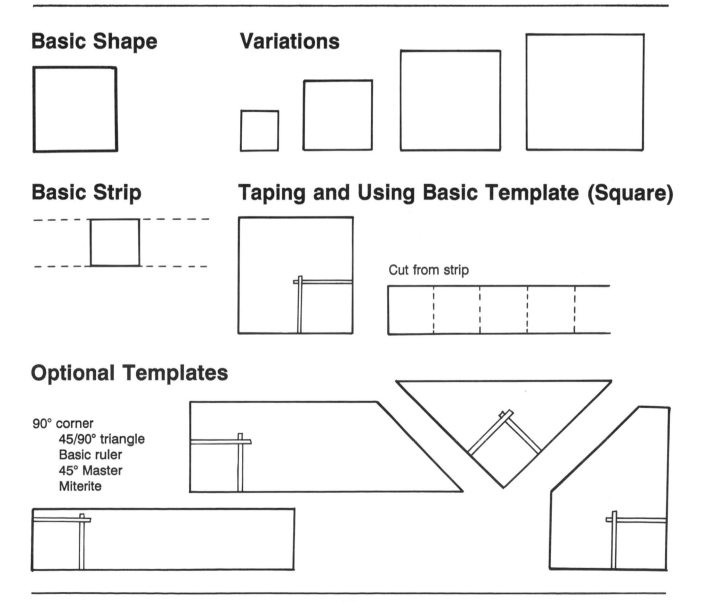

2. Rectangle

Basic Shape   Variations

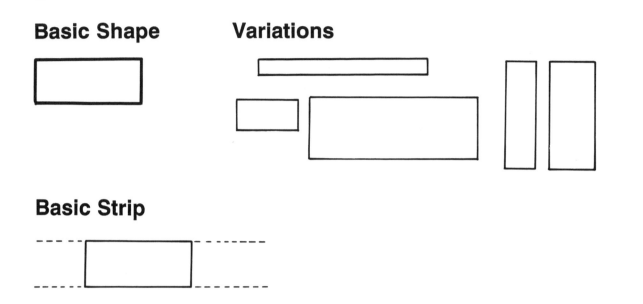

Basic Strip

Taping and Using Basic Template (Square)

Cut from strip

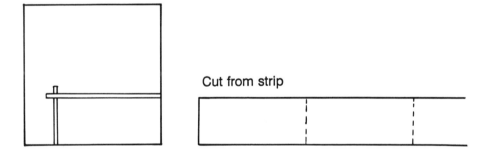

Optional Templates

90° corner
    Basic ruler
    Miterite
    45° Master
    45/90° triangle

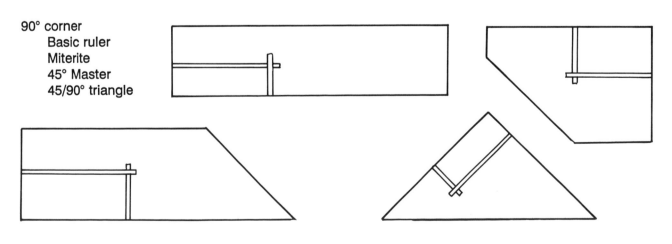

3. Diamond–45°, 60°

Basic Shape

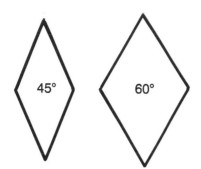

Variations

Basic Strip

Taping and Using Basic Template (Diamond)

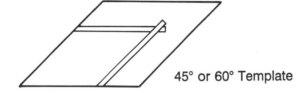

45° or 60° Template

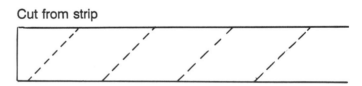

Cut from strip

Optional Templates

45° angle
    45° Master
    Miterite
    45° triangle
60° angle
    60° triangle

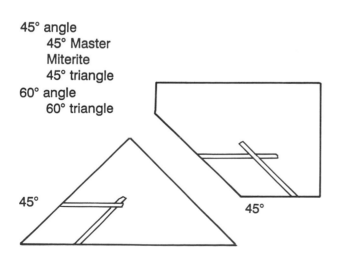

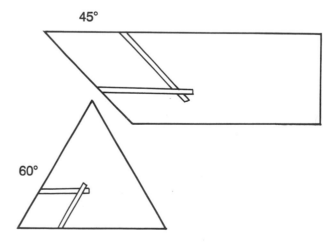

4. Long Diamond–45°, 60°

Basic Shape

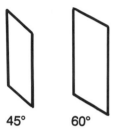

45°   60°

Variations

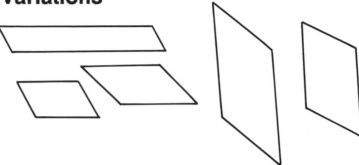

Basic Strip

Taping and Using Basic Template (Diamond)

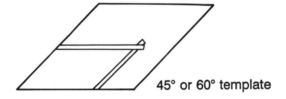

45° or 60° template

Cut from strip

Optional Templates

45° angle
    45° Master
    Miterite
    45° triangle
60° angle
    60° triangle

45°   60°

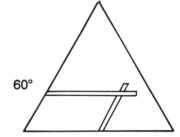

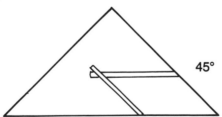

5. Triangle–45°/90°

Basic Shape

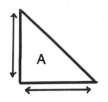

Straight grain
on short sides

Straight grain
on long side

Variations

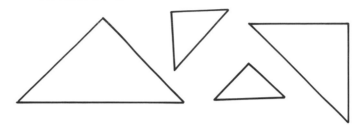

Basic Strip

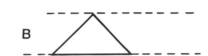

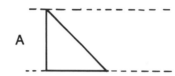

Taping and Using Basic Template (45° Triangle)

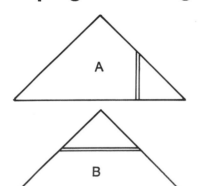

Cut from strip

A

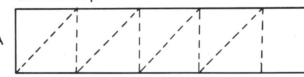

B

Optional Templates

45° corners
    Miterite
    45° diamond
    Squares, cut in half (makes 2 per square)
90° corners
    45° Master
    Miterite
    Square

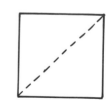

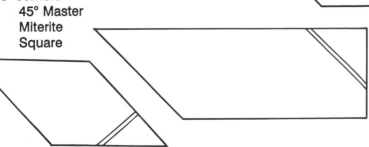

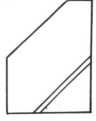

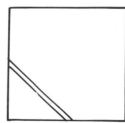

6. Triangle–Equilateral, 60°

Basic Shape

Variations

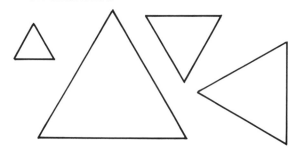

Basic Strip

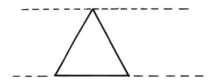

Taping and Using Basic Template (60° Triangle)

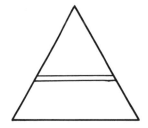

Cut from strip

Optional Templates

60° Diamond

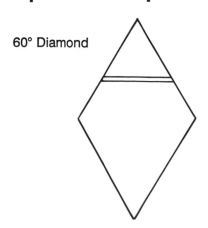

7. Anvil—45°, 60°

Basic Shape

Variations

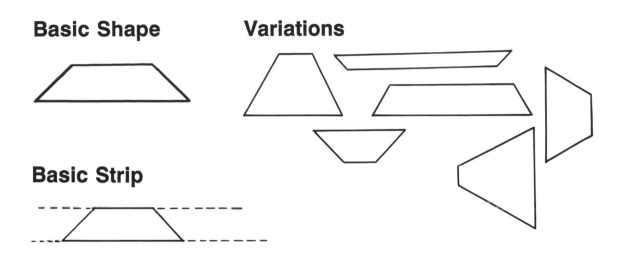

Basic Strip

Taping and Using Basic Template (45° or 60° Triangle)

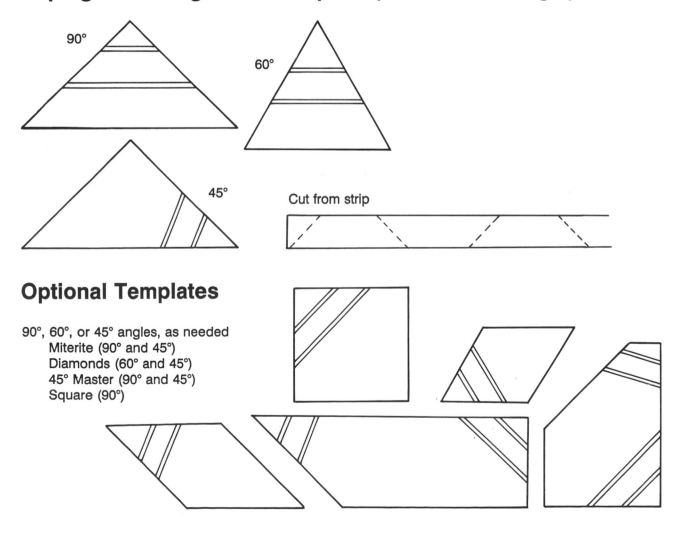

90°

60°

45°

Cut from strip

Optional Templates

90°, 60°, or 45° angles, as needed
  Miterite (90° and 45°)
  Diamonds (60° and 45°)
  45° Master (90° and 45°)
  Square (90°)

8. Shoe–45°, 60°

Basic Shape

Variations

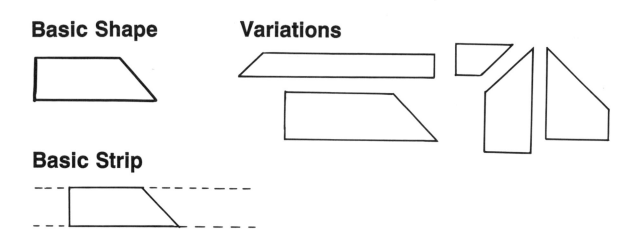

Basic Strip

Taping and Using Basic Templates (45° or 60° Triangle)

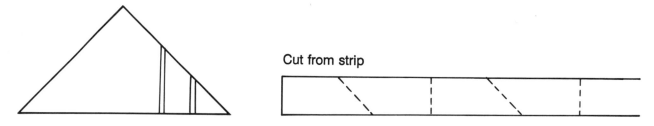

Cut from strip

Optional Templates

45° Angle
　　Miterite
　　45° Master
　　45° diamond
60° angle
　　60° diamond

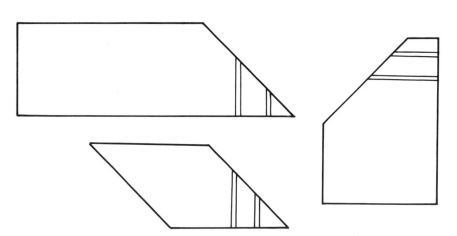

9. Candle

Basic Shape

Variations

Basic Strip

Taping and Using Basic Template (45° Triangles)

Cut from strip

Cut #1   Cut #2

Optional Templates

45° angle
  Miterite
  45° Master

Square
Hexagon
Diamond

Use to cut corner, as needed

Use to cut end

Plus

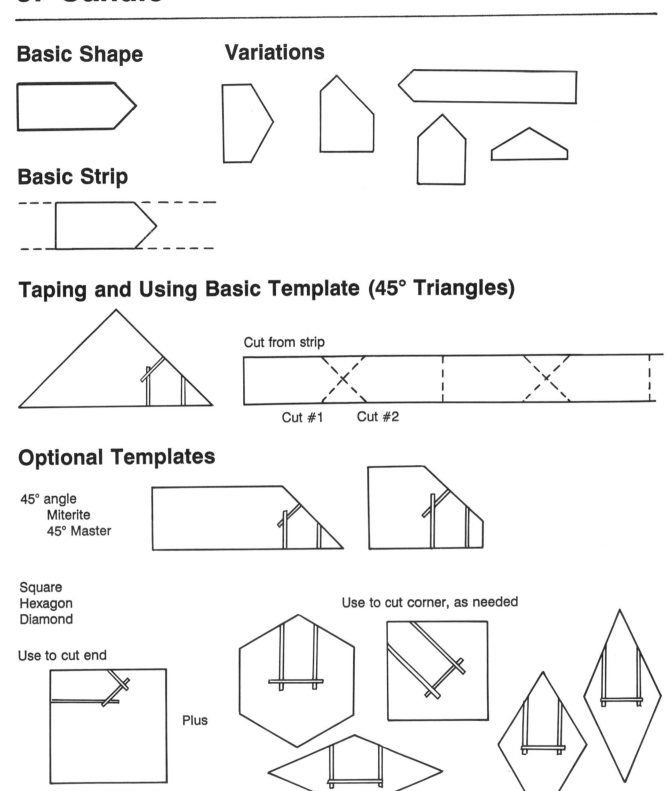

10. Hexagon

Basic Shape   ## Variations

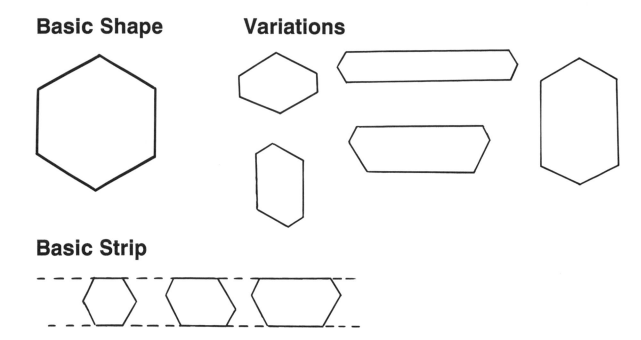

Basic Strip

Taping and Using Basic Template (Hexagon)

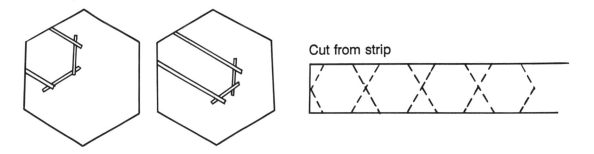

Cut from strip

Optional Templates

60° diamond
60° triangle

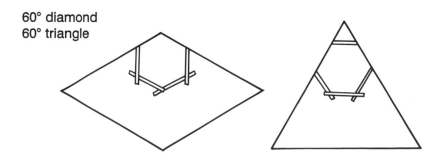

11. Two-ended Candle, 90° Ends

Basic Shape   Variations

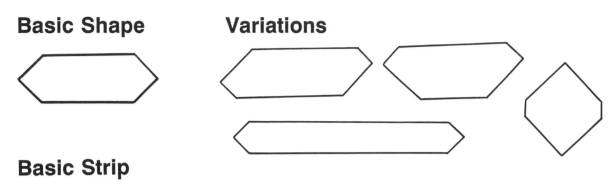

Basic Strip

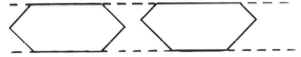

Taping and Using Basic Template (45° Triangle)

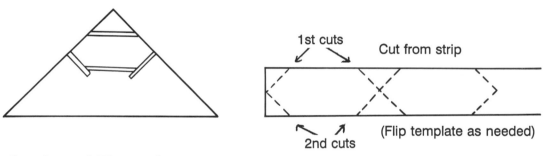

1st cuts   Cut from strip

(Flip template as needed)

2nd cuts

Optional Templates

90° angles
   Square
   Basic ruler
   Miterite
   45° Master

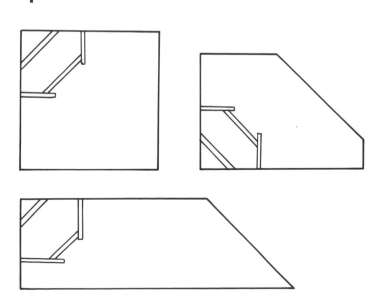

12. Octagon

Basic Shape

Variations

Basic Strip

Taping and Using Basic Template (Square)

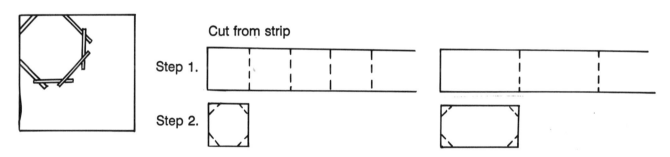

Cut from strip

Step 1.

Step 2.

Optional Templates

90° angle
    45°/90° triangle
    Basic ruler
    Miterite
    45° Master

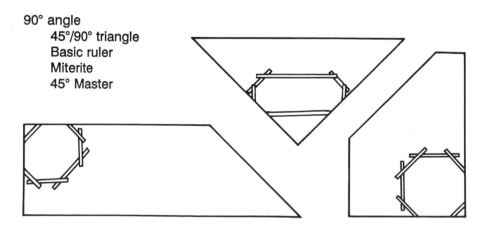

13. Lop-eared Square

Basic Shape

Variations

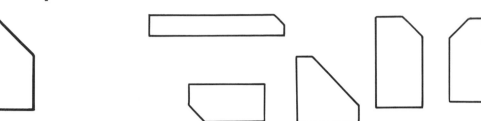

Basic Strip

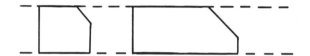

Taping and Using Basic Template (Miterite)

Cut from strip

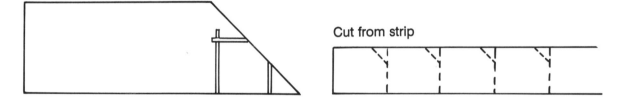

Optional Templates

45° diamond

    OR

Square or rectangle
Plus
45° diamond or 45° Master to cut corner

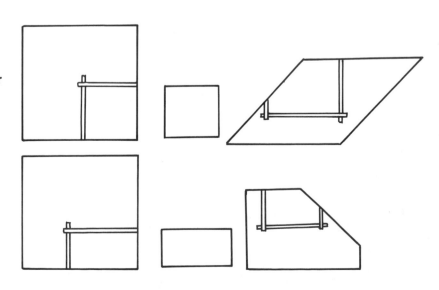

14. Gemstone

Basic Shape

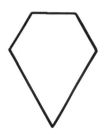

Variations

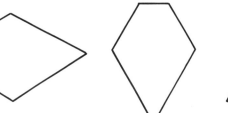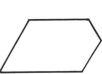

Basic Strip

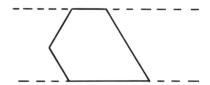

Taping and Using Basic Template (60° Diamond)

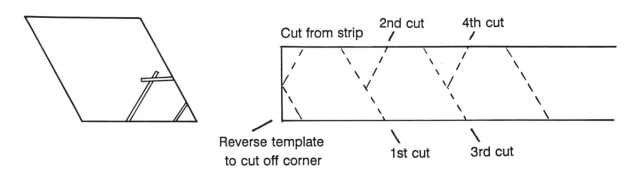

Cut from strip   2nd cut   4th cut

Reverse template
to cut off corner   1st cut   3rd cut

Optional Templates

60° triangle

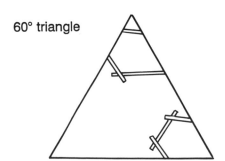

15. Circle

Basic Shape

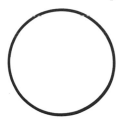

Basic Strip

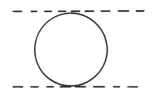

Using Basic Template (Circle, No Taping Needed)

 Cut from strip

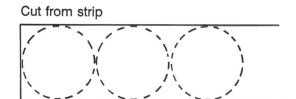

Options

Cut circles from heavy template plastic. Cut no more than four layers of fabric at one time. Work carefully as cutter will easily slice plastic template.

Notes

1. Most circular pieces are appliquéd so seam allowances may be larger than ¼". Use the next larger size circle than the pattern. The cardboard pressing template will determine the final shape (see Chapter 5).

2. Cutting around circles on multiple layers is not as neat as cutting straight lines. With a little practice, though, you will soon become quite comfortable with it.

16. Crescent (for Double Wedding Ring)

Basic Shape

Variations

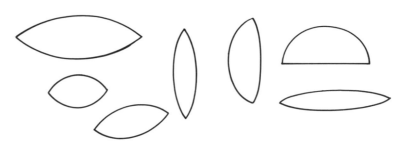

Basic Strip

Taping and Using Basic Template (Double Wedding Ring)

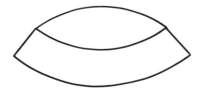

Cut from strip

Optional Templates for Variations

Circle
Drunkard's Path

Note: Cut shapes do not have to be exact if piece is to be appliquéd. Final shape will be determined the pressing template. (See section on appliqué in Chapter 5.)

Cutting Procedure for Double Wedding Ring, No Taping Needed

If crescent is used for Double Wedding Ring, cut as shown to make best use of fabric.

Use to cut
ring center.

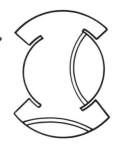

17. Petal

Basic Shape

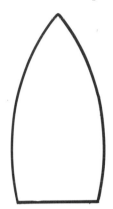

Variations

Basic Strip

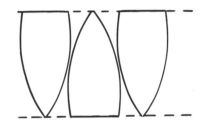

Taping and Using Basic Template (Double Wedding Ring)

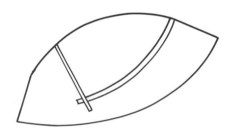

Cut from strip

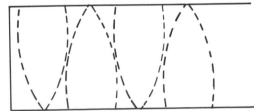

Optional Templates

Circle
Drunkard's Path

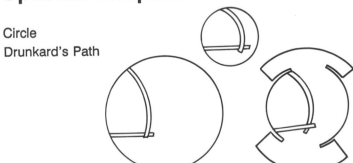

Use optional templates to vary base of petal.

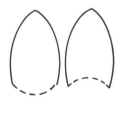

Note: Cut shapes do not have to be exact if piece is to be appliquéd. Final shape will be determined by the pressing template.

18. Archway (for Clamshell)

Basic Shape   Variations

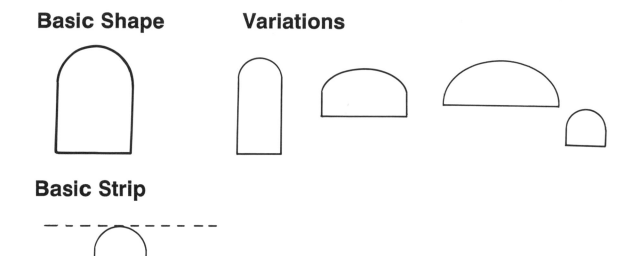

Basic Strip

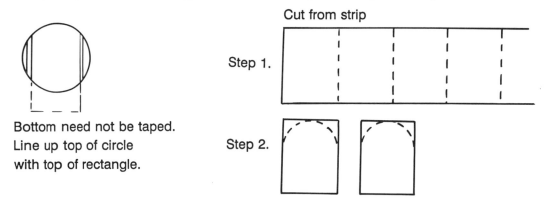

Taping and Using Basic Template (Circle)

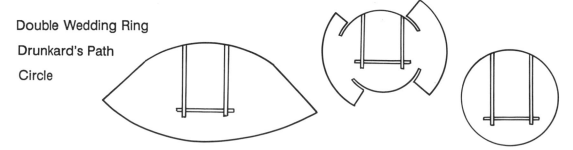

Bottom need not be taped.
Line up top of circle
with top of rectangle.

Cut from strip

Step 1.

Step 2.

Optional Templates

Double Wedding Ring

Drunkard's Path

Circle

Note: Shape of arc does not have to be exact if piece is to be appliquéd. Final shape will be determined by the pressing template.

19. Fan

Basic Shape

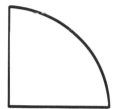

Variations

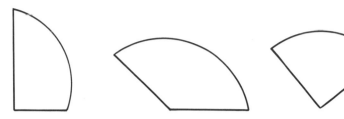

Basic Strip

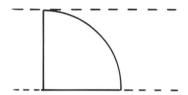

Taping and Using Basic Template (Drunkard's Path)

Cut from strip

Step 1.

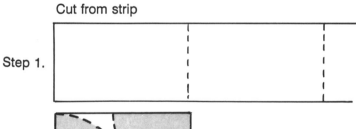

Step 2.

Optional Templates

90° corner
> Square
> Basic Ruler
> Miterite

Plus

Arc
> Double Wedding Ring
> Circle

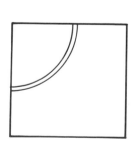
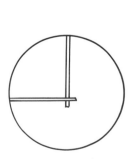
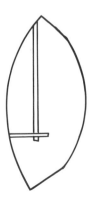

20. Bite

Basic Shape

Variations

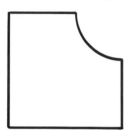
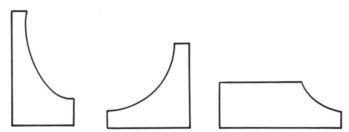

Basic Strip

Taping and Using Basic Template (Drunkard's Path)

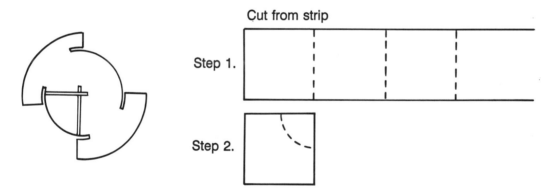

Cut from strip

Step 1.

Step 2.

Optional Templates

Circle
Double Wedding Ring

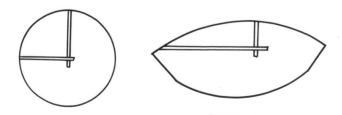

21. Ax-Head

Basic Shape

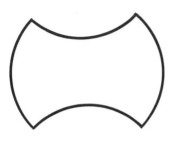

Variations

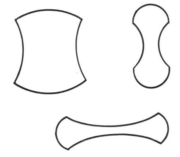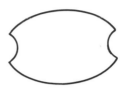

Basic Strip

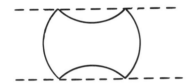

Taping and Using Basic Template (Circles)

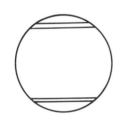

Use in Step 1

Cut from strip

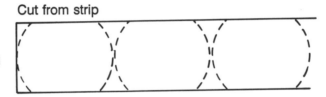

Use in Step 2

Optional Templates

Drunkard's Path
Double Wedding Ring

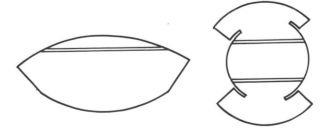

22. Cone, Pointed End (20 per circle)

Basic Shape

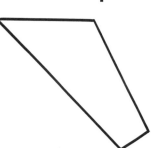

Variations

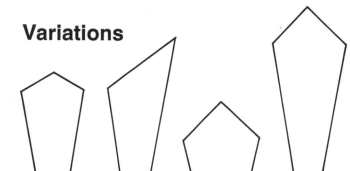

Basic Strip

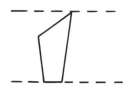

Taping and Using Basic Template (Miterite, Jr. and Dresden Plate)

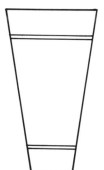

Use for Step 1

Cut from strip

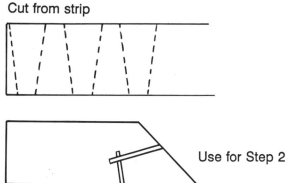

Use for Step 2

Optional Templates

Basic ruler
Miterite
Square

Plus

Square, diamond or triangle
as needed for top shape

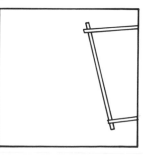

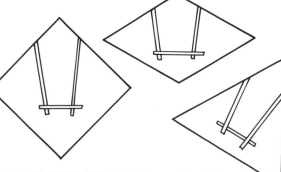

Note: Suggestion for cone tip can also be used with shape #23, 10 per circle cone.

23. Cone, Arc End (10 per circle)

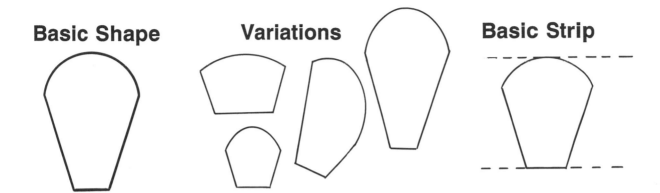

Basic Shape **Variations** **Basic Strip**

Taping and Using Basic Template (Circle and Dresden Plate)

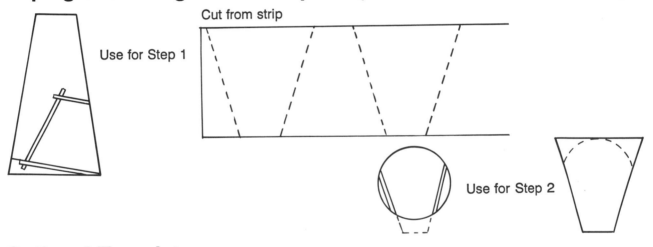

Use for Step 1

Cut from strip

Use for Step 2

Optional Templates

Basic Ruler
Miterite
Square

Plus

Drunkard's Path or Double Wedding Ring
  as needed for top shape

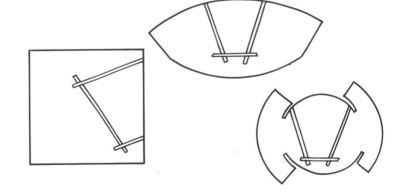

Notes:
1. Shape of arc does not have to be exact if piece is to be appliquéd. Final shape will be determined by the pressing template.

2. Suggestion for cone top (arc shape) can also be used with shape #22, 20 per circle cone.

24. Arc Pieces (for Double Wedding Ring)

Basic Shape

Variations

Using Basic Template (Double Wedding Ring; No Taping Needed)

Step 1. Cut arc

Step 2. Cut pieces as needed (see templates, Appendix C):

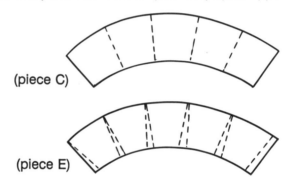

(piece C)

(piece E)

Basic Strip for Variations

Optional Templates for Variations

Basic Ruler
Miterite
Square

Plus

Drunkard's Path, circles,
   or any template needed
   for top and bottom shapes

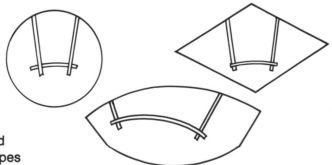

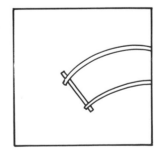

Note: Shape of arc does not have to be exact if piece is to be appliquéd. Final shape will be determined by the pressing template.

25. Single Arc (for Double Wedding Ring)

Basic Shape

Variations

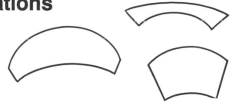

Using Basic Template (Double Wedding Ring; No Taping Needed)

Step 1. Cut arc

Step 2. Trim ¼″ from both ends

Basic Strip for Variations

Optional Templates for Variations

Basic Ruler
Miterite
Square

Plus

Circles, Drunkard's Path,
  or any template needed
  for top and bottom shapes

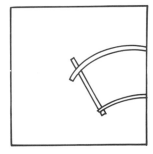

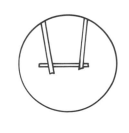

(Bottom Shape)

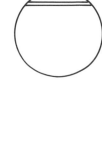

Top

Bottom

26. Odd-Shaped Triangle with a 90° Angle

Basic Shape

Variations

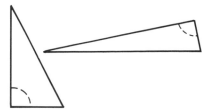

Basic Strip

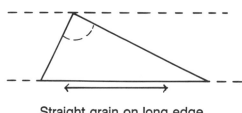

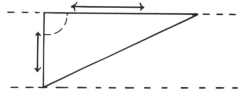

Straight grain on long edge

Straight grain on two shorter edges

Taping and Using Basic Template (Basic Ruler)

Option 1: If you want straight grain on long edge of shape

Cut from strip

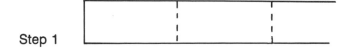

Option 2: If you want straight grain on two shorter edges of shape

Step 1

Step 2

Optional Templates

90° Angle
   Miterite
   Square
   45° Master
   45° triangle

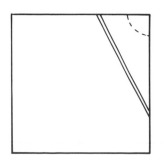
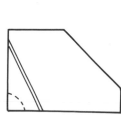
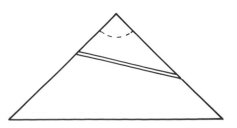

27. Odd-Shaped Triangle with a 60° Angle

Basic Shape

Variations

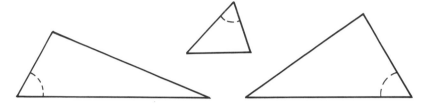

Basic Strip

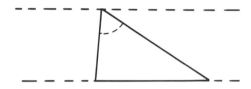

Taping and Using Basic Template (60° Triangle)

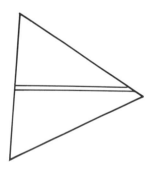

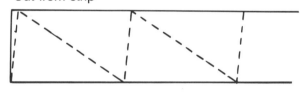

Cut from strip

Optional Templates

60° Diamond

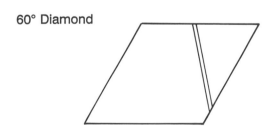

Note: Straight grain will be on edge opposite 60° angle. To place straight grain on any other edge, refer to Shape #29 (Figuring Out Unusual Shapes).

28. Odd-Shaped Triangle with a 45° Angle

Basic Shape

Variations

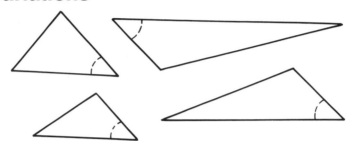

Basic Strip

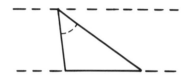

Taping and Using Basic Template (Miterite)

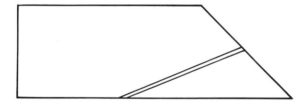

Cut from strip

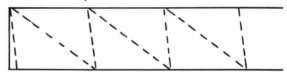

Optional Templates

45° triangle
45° diamond

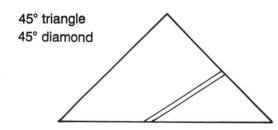

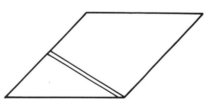

Note: Straight grain will be on edge opposite 45° angle. To place straight grain on any other edge, refer to shape #29 (Figuring Out Unusual Shapes).

29. Figuring Out Unusual Shapes

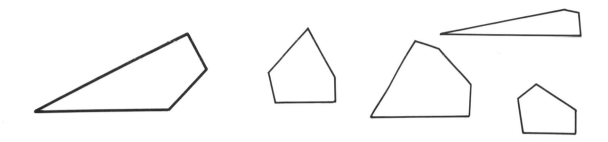

Occasionally you'll want to cut a piece that simply does not match any template available. Good news! It can still be rotary-cut with your templates. Here's how:

Look for any angle that matches an angle of your templates. This will give you two cutting edges.

If no angle can be found, then any piece with straight edges can be rotary-cut, one side at a time. Just follow this procedure:

1. One cut can be made by cutting a strip (this will be the straight grain of the piece).

2. Now place template over pattern and tape the template along as many straight edges as needed to cut the other sides of the shape.

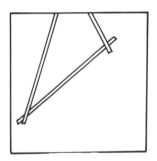 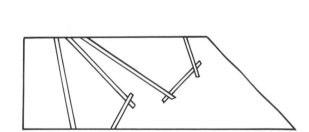 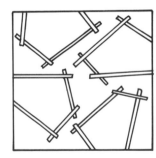

3. Cut pieces from strips.

Example of Cutting Sequence

 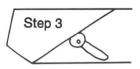

 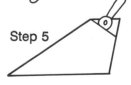 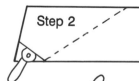

Did you figure this one out? You did? Then you deserve a gold star because it's the hardest one of all.

30. Clipped Points

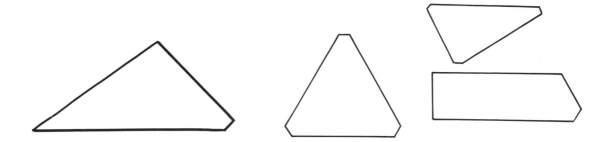

Many pattern pieces have the points clipped off. This saves a lot of guesswork as it creates two precisely matched corners to sew together. If your seams are a consistent scant ¼", your finished angles will delight you. They will be perfect!

To rotary-cut these clipped-off points, just tape your template along any straight edge.

This step is worth it!

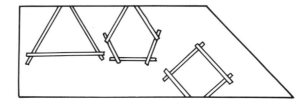

4

PLANNING YOUR QUILT

Basic Construction Plan

Step 1. Preparation (covered in this chapter).
   A. Choose size, color, and design of quilt. Record information on Play-Plan.
   B. Purchase fabric. Preshrink.
   C. Gather all supplies and equipment needed.

Step 2. Cutting
   A. Make or tape all cutting templates. Refer to Speed-Cutting instructions in Chapter 2 as needed.
   B. Cut all pieces for quilt top.

Step 3. Sewing
   A. Piece center portion of quilt top as instructions indicate. Refer to Chapter 5, Basic Construction Techniques, for specific sewing techniques.
   B. Add borders.

Margaret, Barbara, and Helen at a modern quilting bee

Step 4. Finishing
   A. Mark quilting lines, if desired.
   B. Baste and quilt.
   C. Finish edges.

Choosing Your Project

Now that you've practiced some of these fun and fast techniques, you'll want to use them. Start with one of the 20 quilts in this book. Sound easy? Well, if you're anything like me, you can spend weeks just deciding which one to make first, because you really want to do them all! I try hard to get over that hurdle fast, realizing that in all that time of indecision, I could have made several quilts.

A Few Hints

- If you're new to the rotary cutter, start with a quilt labeled "Beginner."

- A quilt with one or two pattern pieces is easier and faster to cut out than one with a lot of pieces.

- A hand-pieced quilt such as the "Grandmother's Flower Garden" takes longer to stitch. However, it is a great "take-along" project and allows you to be with family and friends while you piece, rather than holed up with your sewing machine.

- Special techniques, such as set-ins, curves, six-points, and appliqué, will take a bit longer than straight-line piecing and joining. Of course, this matters only if time is important. If you're enjoying the project, time will seem to pass too quickly, anyhow.

- Go with your instincts. If one quilt really jumps out and says "Do me!"—then, do it! Remember, this is your hobby and if you

Carol and Sue S. cutting out new quilts

make your quilts with love and happiness, others will feel it, too.

Once you have chosen which quilt to make, it's time to choose the colors and then the fabrics.

Using the Design Pages

Each of the 20 quilts in this book has a design page, which you can use to select colors. Make as many copies of this page as you want. Get a good assortment of colored pencils and some #2 lead pencils. Now start playing with color! You can have hours of fun and you'll be astonished at the many variations you'll come up with!

When you decide which quilt you want to make, cut a copy of the design to the size you want. Copy the borders and add them to the design. This way, you'll have a sketch of the entire quilt.

Border suggestions have been included, but do create your own if you like. Borders can be fun! My favorite is a narrow "framing" strip used as the first border. I use one of my darker fabrics and cut it 1½″ wide (including ¼″ seam allowance) for small quilts and 2″ wide for medium and large quilts. My last border is usually the widest and always my favorite print from the quilt.

Now count the number of pieces needed of each color and shape. Record all of this on a Play-Plan (see later in this chapter and Appendix C), and you're ready to go.

Bow Tie (Quilt 3). Diana Hylton. Plaid and black, 62″ × 86″.

Nighttime (Quilt 11).
Nancy Smith. Black,
magenta, and aqua,
86" × 106".

Peacock (Quilt 13).
Suzette Harris. Fuchsia
and teal, 86" × 110".

Nosegay (Quilt 20). Susan Reisser. Multicolor, 91" × 108".

Clamshell (Quilt 15). Donna Poster, quilting by Lillie Spencer. Black, mauve, and teal, 57" × 72".

Magnolias (Quilt 14). Sharon Chambers. Multicolor, 68" × 97".

Dresden Plate (Quilt 2). Donna Poster. Black and earth tones, 60" × 72".

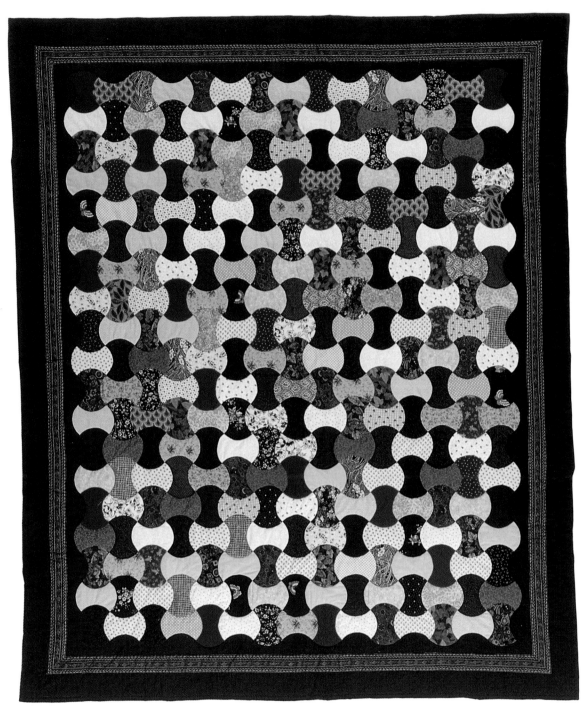

Always Friends (Quilt 12). Sue Miller. Black, gray, and red, 39" × 53".

Opposite page (top):
Indian Star (Quilt 8). Trina Rehkemper. Green and cream, 60" × 84".

Opposite page (bottom):
Texas Trellis (Quilt 5). Barbara Tulloch. Wine, green, and blue, 84" × 104".

Flower Basket (Quilt 18). Helen Oelkrug. Blue and mauve, 52" × 70".

Color

Color selection is one of the most important parts of creating a beautiful quilt. It's also the scariest, because the rules we've learned for picking clothing are not the same as for quilts and even the color experts don't agree on the rules! To add to the confusion, some of the most beautiful quilts I've ever seen break all the rules!

So where in the world is a mere beginner supposed to start? First of all, look in quilt magazines, books, calendars, and at nature for color schemes you like. You'll be surprised at how differently you'll see the world around you.

Ask for help from other quiltmakers, teachers, and store owners. In my classes, we have "show and tell" times to learn how colors and prints work in various combinations. Following are a few guidelines that my students find helpful.

Color Family

First, pick one or two main colors and one or more accent colors. Be flexible, though—you may change your mind when you spot a piece of fabric you "have to have."

An easy way to start is to pick a fabric with the look you want. Study it. Are the colors bright and clear? Or grayed earth tones? Whatever the colors, keep all other colors in the family. A bright sailor blue added to a pile of teal, salmon, and taupe will screech like nails across a blackboard. But the same blue with a bright red and sunshine yellow will be terrific.

Look at the proportions of the colors—which stand out? Which are small highlights? Is the print so tiny it's almost a solid? Is it a bold geometric? A frilly, fussy print?

Use the answers to these questions as a starting point.

When putting fabrics together to create a lovely quilt, there are as many different sets of rules as there are "experts." The soft, subtle quilt that warms Sue's heart is simply dull and bland to Nancy. And the bold, vibrating colors Nancy enjoys are garish to Sue.

Trina and Sue M. arranging Sue's Bow Tie squares

Color Values

Value is the lightness and darkness of the fabrics. The contrasts and shadings created by the values you choose will determine the character of your quilt.

Look through pages of quilt designs and note the light, medium, and dark values and what they do to the quilts. In general, for a strong, bold look, use high-contrast colors: a very light next to a very dark (your quilt will take on the color of the dark fabric).

For a subdued, quiet look, use low-contrast colors. To create a dark but quiet quilt, use darks and mediums, but no lights. For a light but quiet look, use lights, mediums, and no darks.

In a way, there are no mediums. If you put a medium fabric next to a light, there will be a contrast. If you want to soften this contrast, insert fabrics that "shade" the two together.

If you like the look of a particular quilt, it can best be achieved by following the values shown in the picture. Do feel free to change them, though. Experimenting is fun.

Barbara, Susan, and Helen picking fabrics

Prints and Stripes

The surest way to achieve an interesting quilt is to use a wide variety of print sizes and styles, including an occasional solid.

For a dramatic, bold look, use all solids. Magnificent quilts are made with a repetition of one or two blocks using just two high-contrast solids.

Soft prints and low contrast will produce a lovely, subdued, mellow quilt. (Yes, you can use lots of tiny prints together.)

Cut up large prints at random for an exciting sense of movement. The pieces will not be exactly alike, yet will definitely feel like parts of a whole. Don't be afraid of ending up with headless pheasants and finless fish—you're sure to like the results of experimenting this way.

Don't bother about tiny bits of odd color in a fabric. If you're making a maroon and blue quilt and that perfect navy print has tiny bits of rust in the print, use it. When the quilt is done, your eye will change the rust to maroon.

Some prints create illusions of stripes when viewed from a distance. These usually require no special cutting for small pieces. But for borders and lattice strips, it is important to have the stripe effect line up with the long edge. To achieve this, simply cut these long edges parallel to the selvage and the design will fall right into place.

You may, at times, find a design with areas or motifs you would like to highlight. These will have to be cut individually. (Be sure to buy extra fabric to account for the waste.) Be aware of the top and bottom of this motif in relation to your finished quilt. (The transparent templates are perfect for centering these special prints).

Stay Flexible

When you're making a quilt, things happen along the way; you need more of a certain fabric and it's no longer available; the test was wrong and it turned out to be a boy; Aunt Ruth wants a purple quilt and you hate purple. The list is endless.

Relax. Let's consider some alternatives. That fabric you need—could you substitute something close to it? Use a coordinating rather than a matching fabric in the border? Make a lap throw, pillow, or tote bag of this piece and start over on another quilt?

You can give the blue quilt to a baby girl, but people are funny about pink for boys. Put it away for the next girl, take the quickest quilt in the book, and whip a new one up fast.

You can't picture yourself sewing a whole purple quilt? Try to convince Aunt Ruth that a tiny accent of purple would be much more dramatic than a whole quilt of purple. If you can't get out of it, plan a *fast* quilt. After all, this should be enjoyable to you, too.

If everything in the project has gone wrong and you just hate it, fold it up neatly, put it in a box, and hide it on the top shelf of a backroom closet. Then forget about it and start something else. A small project that's a guaranteed success will get you quilting again. Someday you'll find that box, and you'll probably find it works this time. If it still doesn't, give it away.

Developing Color Schemes You'll Love

Select prints because they look good together. The overall design of a fabric will change drastically when cut up in small pieces. A fabric that is ugly on the bolt may be just the thing needed to make your quilt gorgeous.

Black can add excitement (what a shame that we associate it with funerals and villains' hats). Use it to set off brilliant splashes of color. They'll positively vibrate.

Be a little daring if you can. Try an accent of an odd color for a really striking look. Tuck a touch of lavender in a blue quilt. Or a bit of teal in a beige piece.

Don't try to coordinate everything. Study nature and you'll see all sorts of colors together. Part of the beauty of a forest is the many shades of green in the trees, mixed with the highlights of sun and shadows. A beautiful sunset will include yellow, magenta, brilliant blues, purple, and white. What a magnificent quilt that would make!

After selecting your fabrics, walk away, turn, and take a fast look. Did any stand out? If so, use this either as your main color or in small amounts as a highlight. Did any blend together? Then they'll perform as one fabric and you'll lose the effectiveness of both. Did your fabrics please you? Then, go for it!

And don't ignore your backing fabric. A really smashing print will make your quilt interesting and reversible. If you choose a large print, buy an extra repeat per seam so the design can easily be matched. Rely on your own intuition. It helps to have someone play with the fabrics with you, but for a final choice, you are the one who knows best what you like.

Try not to get a set picture of what your quilt will look like. It's virtually impossible to visualize it as it really will be. Pick fabrics that work well together, then enjoy watching your quilt come to life.

Scrap Quilts

To buy or not to buy? Now there's a question!

Quilters love to save their fabric scraps, but the dilemma of how and when to use them keeps most of these scraps in a closet.

Many of the quilts in this book work very nicely with scraps, so I've included some guidelines to help you get going on what will, undoubtedly, be one of your favorite quilts.

It's easy to get hooked on scrap quilts. They're fun to do, and, best of all, they're fun to use. (A scrap quilt can keep a sick child amused for a long time!)

Once you're hooked, though, you start buying piles of different fabrics to add to your stash so you can make great quilts from this growing pile of "scraps."

The first few of these quilts may be somewhat intimidating. Over the years, I've come up with three guidelines for my own use. Eventually you'll want to make your own list, as scrap quilts are all unique.

1. *Lots of contrast.* My lights are very light, so that even my mediums become "darks."
2. *Family unity.* I rarely mix clear, bright colors with gray-tone, earthy colors. It simply doesn't make me feel good. I tend to think of my fabrics as people, and, even though I thoroughly enjoy eccentrics, I do object to a bright red piece screeching its lungs out in the middle of a sedate gathering of soft gray tones.

3. *Don't overcoordinate.* This is probably the hardest thing to keep from doing in a scrap quilt and really separates the right-brain people from the left-brain!

There is one big drawback in doing scrap quilts—they take a lot of time. You can spend hours just playing with the fabric. The cutting, even with my Speedy System, is slower. Several solutions are:

❧ Use quilts with simple pieces such as squares and rectangles.

❧ Do quilts with one piece as in "Always Friends" or "Grandmother's Flower Garden."

❧ Set up an ongoing scrap quilt. I have a template all taped for "Texas Trellis." Everytime I have scraps from something, I cut out six spokes and add them to the box I've set aside for this project. When I sew them together, the cutting and decisions will all be done!

Now that you have chosen your project and color scheme, it's time to fill in your Play-Plan.

Using the Play-Plan

This Play-Plan is simpler than the one in my book *Speed-Cut Quilts* because the quilts in this book are actually just one enormous block. My first Play-Plan, in *Speed-Cut Quilts,* had to allow for the use of several different blocks.

Use this as a guide for gathering the necessary information. Make a separate copy for each quilt you make. Fill it all in and on the reverse side, attach a picture of the finished quilt, plus comments on the events of the times, both historical and personal.

Your great-grandchildren will love it!

Filling in the Play-Plan (Appendix C)

1. Copy the following:
   Border (Appendix A)
   Instructions page (20 Quilts)
   Design page (20 Quilts)
   Backing layout (Appendix A)
2. Fill in Play-Plan:

A.

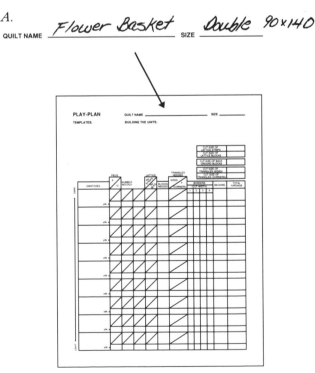

B. Paste on drawing of "templates":

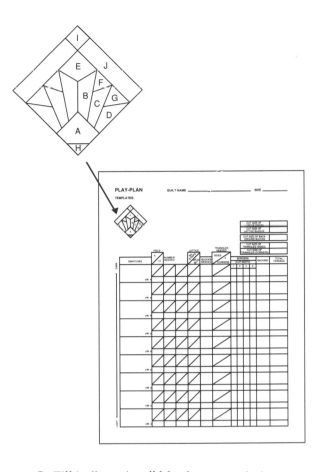

D. Paste on swatches. You can pencil in your colors first, then take your Play-Plan to the fabric store. When you return, paste on your swatches.

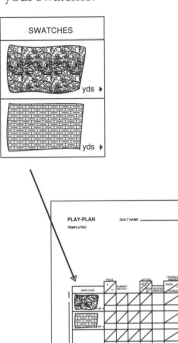

C. Fill in "cut sizes" blocks as needed:

CUT SIZE OF TRIANGLES (SIDES)	12×12
CUT SIZE OF TRIANGLES (CORNERS)	9×9

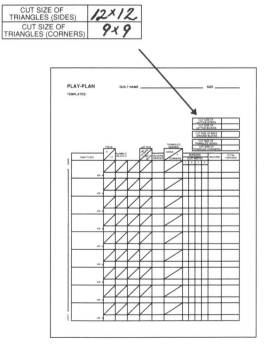

E. Fill in piece and number needed next to swatch of fabric being used:

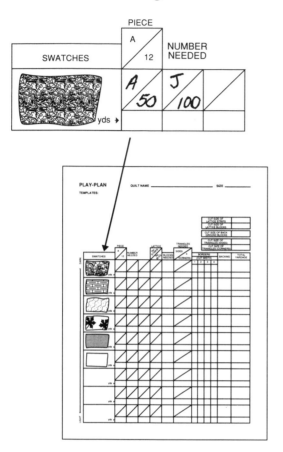

F. Fill in blocks, triangles, borders, backing, and other units, as needed:

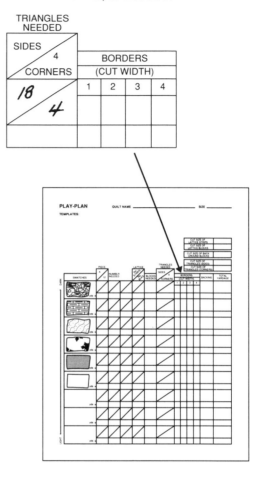

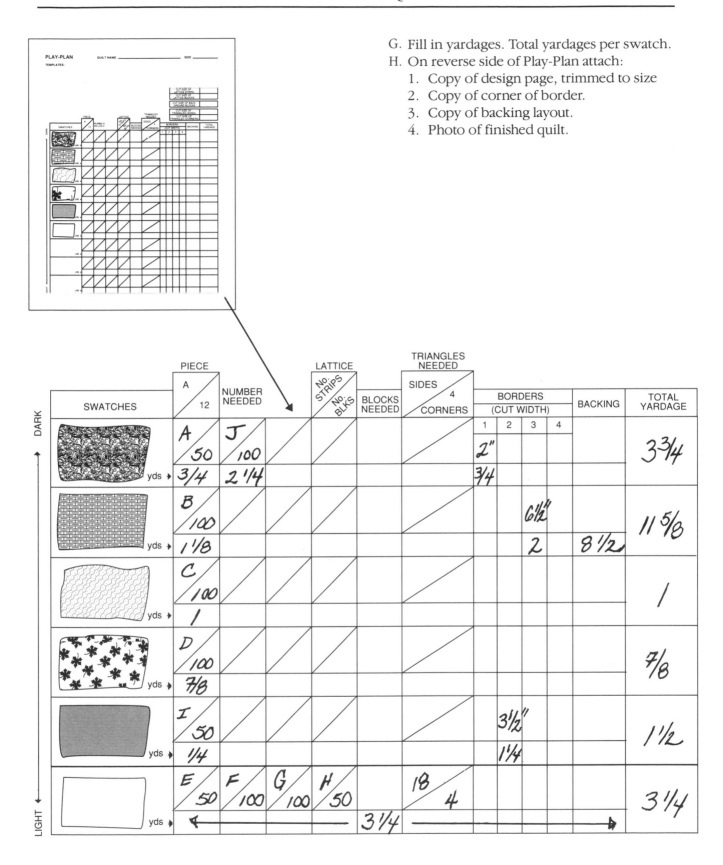

G. Fill in yardages. Total yardages per swatch.
H. On reverse side of Play-Plan attach:
   1. Copy of design page, trimmed to size
   2. Copy of corner of border.
   3. Copy of backing layout.
   4. Photo of finished quilt.

SWATCHES	PIECE A / 12	NUMBER NEEDED	LATTICE No. STRIPS / No. BLKS	BLOCKS NEEDED	TRIANGLES NEEDED SIDES / 4 / CORNERS	BORDERS (CUT WIDTH) 1	2	3	4	BACKING	TOTAL YARDAGE
(dark swatch) yds →	A / 50 / 3/4	J / 100 / 2 1/4				2" 3/4					3 3/4
(brick swatch) yds →	B / 100 / 1 1/8						6 1/2" 2			8 1/2	11 5/8
(wavy swatch) yds →	C / 100 / 1										1
(floral swatch) yds →	D / 100 / 7/8										7/8
(gray swatch) yds →	I / 50 / 1/4					3 1/2" 1 1/4					1 1/2
(white swatch) yds →	E / 50	F / 100	G / 100	H / 50	18 / 4						3 1/4

←————— 3 1/4 —————→

DARK ↑   LIGHT ↓

Buying the Fabric

Now that you've decided on size, layout, and general color scheme and have made a Play-Plan, (see page 212), it's time to buy fabric. Take your Play-Plan to the store.

One hundred percent cotton is the sturdiest, most durable fabric for quilts. It also has a slight nap, which helps keep the pieces together while stitching.

Buy enough. Fabrics can disappear from a store overnight and never be available again. Many a quilter has become frustrated and discouraged when she finds that the piece she's run out of is no longer available. Better to buy extra and if you then have leftovers, you can make marvelous quilts with the scraps.

For this same reason, if you see a fabric you really like, buy it. Manufacturers often produce only one run of a fabric. You may never find it again. How much to buy? My rules of thumb are: (1) if I'm absolutely wild about it, I'll buy at least 2½ yards (enough for an unpieced border); (2) if it's really super background fabric, I'll buy 5 or 6 yards; and (3) if it's a nice accent piece, but a little goes a long way, I'll get 1 or 2 yards.

To organize all the information for your quilt, see Using the Play-Plan, earlier in this chapter. If stripes are used in your blocks, consider the waste. You'll need ¼ to ⅓ yard or more extra fabric.

The yardages in this book are based on 44″ fabric and allow extra for shrinkage and waste.

Store fabric neatly, preferably in boxes and according to color. Avoid airtight plastic bags, which will eventually cause your fabric to deteriorate.

Preparing Your Fabric for Quilting

Prewashing is recommended to preshrink the fabric and remove excess sizing. The grain is then reliable just as it comes from the dryer. It has the extra advantage of washing out any excess dye from the darker fabrics, and you'll have a washable quilt when finished.

Snip a little ¼″ triangle off each of the four corners of your fabric before tossing it in the washing machine. This cuts down on raveling and tangling. Wash lights and darks separately.

Try a light spray of fabric sizing when ironing—it's much easier to get the wrinkles out. It also adds a bit more body, making those small pieces easier to work with. If you're working with a lot of bias cuts, this is a "must."

After laundering, trim all selvages off before cutting.

Supplies

The following supplies are quite common in today's quilting scene. Ask for them at your local sewing or quilting store. If they do not stock an item, perhaps they can order it for you.

If you are not close to a store, look in the Supply List at the back of this book. I have included a list of fine mail-order sources there.

Rotary cutting equipment. See Chapter 1 for more information.

Fabric. 100% cotton. Fabric purchasing and preparation are discussed in detail earlier in this chapter.

¼″ quilter's tape. A narrow, non-residue tape to use on your cutting templates.

Template plastic. Used in cutting Double Wedding Ring.

Fine, permanent marking pen. For marking on template plastic. My favorite is the

Pigma Pen as it can be used to write on muslin labels, too.

Spray starch. Helps on any fabrics that lose their body after laundering.

Long, large head quilting pins. You won't know how you lived without them!

Silk pins. These are long, extra-fine dressmaker pins that glide easily through your fabric.

Sequin pins. Many of my students prefer these very short pins for appliqué.

Safety pins. Nickel-plated, 1″ long; about 350 will baste a double-bed-size quilt.

Sewing thread. My favorite is a large cone of natural-colored thread. I wind a dozen bobbins with it and I'm set for hours. You may use odds and ends of good-quality thread for piecing, as it does not have to match the fabric. You will also need thread to match backing fabric (for machine-quilting only) and to match outer border (which becomes the binding).

Fine sewing thread. Silk or silk-finish for hand appliqué. Must match or blend with the fabric.

Pearl cotton #3. Only for tying quilts; it has sheen, is washable, and is easy to handle. Use two or three strands.

Invisible thread. Machine quilting only.

Quilting thread. Hand quilting only.

Quilting needles. Hand quilting only. Use "betweens" size 8 to 10; the smaller the needle, the shorter the stitch!

Hand sewing needle. For appliqué and handsewing, use sharps, or milliners, size 10.

Large darning needle or **curved upholstery needle.** For tying quilts.

Lightweight cardboard. Use as pressing templates. Any of the following will work: manila folders, index cards, poster boards, or cereal boxes.

Walking foot or **even-feed foot.** Machine quilting only. It will feed the three thicknesses of your quilt evenly.

Darning foot. Machine quilting only. Use for free-form quilting.

Common sewing tools. Scissors, seam ripper, thimble, etc. No list here, as everyone has her favorites.

Thimble. Try them all till you find one you like. It will be worth the effort.

Iron. I prefer a steam iron used gently.

Quilting stencils. Use to draw quilting lines on quilt. Purchase these or create your own from lightweight plastic sheets.

Marking pen (water soluble). Needed only to mark quilting lines. If all your quilting follows seam lines, this is not needed.

Batting. Look for the word "bonded." It holds up well in the washing machine and needs very little quilting. The low-loft seems to be my customers' favorite and is the easiest to hand-quilt.

Flannel or fleece. Often used as batting for clothing or table coverings.

Lap frame. Only for hand quilting small areas at a time.

Hoop or **floor frame.** Only for hand quilting whole quilts.

Bicycle clips. Hold quilt tightly rolled for machine quilting.

Quilt label. Sign your quilt. Tell the world you're proud of it!

Dressmaker carbon. For appliqué only. Used to trace the pressing templates.

5

BASIC CONSTRUCTION TECHNIQUES

Sewing Skills

My beginning students always ask, "How do I know when to rip it out?" I tell them the following:

Be as accurate as you can while still having fun. Remember, this is your hobby, not your job, and your first quilts will not hang in the Smithsonian, so don't spend time ripping out every seam that's not a perfect match. If you enjoy your first quilt, you'll make more of them, and as you do, you'll get better at it.

If you need to do some easing to get seams to match, don't worry. The quilting takes up a lot of errors in the "puffies."

Know what is really important and pay attention to that. For example, learn to maintain a scant 1/4″ seam allowance. Careful cutting is important. Learn to adjust your sewing machine to maintain good tension. Use a small size (70/10) sewing machine needle for piecing, and change it every time you start a new quilt. Use good quality fabrics and thread.

Pay attention to these things and you'll be amazed at how easily it all fits together!

Trina machine piecing

Machine Piecing

A balanced tension is important. Your stitching should not draw up the fabric (if it does, your tension is too tight or your stitches too long). You should not see the bobbin thread from the top side.

For piecing, use a medium to small stitch (12–15 stitches per inch). There is no backstitching at the ends of most of the seams, and these small stitches will not pull out.

Use a fine to medium machine needle size (70/10 to 80/12). Change the needle often: it will make a difference in the quality of your stitching.

Poke through your box of machine accessories and find the single-hole needle plate (Fig. 5-1) to replace that wide-hole (zigzag) plate. You'll have better control of your fabric with the single-hole plate. Don't set your machine on zigzag. If you don't have a single-hole needle plate, decenter the needle to the left or right, but remember that doing so changes the width of your seam

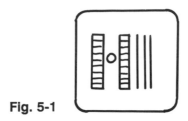

Fig. 5-1

allowance. Or tape an index card over the zigzag needle plate, cutting holes for the feed dogs. Lower an unthreaded needle into the card. Then enlarge the hole slightly.

The ¼" Seam

Finding and maintaining a perfect ¼" seam will make your piecing time enjoyable. Pieces fit together; ripping is almost nonexistent. To find a reference point on your sewing machine, mark a line ¼" from the edge of a piece of paper. Insert the machine needle into the line. Drop the presser foot. Find an easy sighting at the edge of the paper (the edge of the foot, the presser foot opening, etc.). You may want to use masking tape or a seam guide. On some machines, you can decenter the needle so that the needle falls ¼" away from the sighting you choose. If you have a computerized machine, make sure you return to this setting every time you turn on the machine again. Learn to guide the cut edge of your fabric along this sighting, and you won't have to spend time marking your seams.

About that ¼" seam—make it a scant ¼" (Fig. 5-2). There's a bit of loft in the fabric at any seam, creating a shortage in the size of that piece. It may seem insignificant, but a block with eight pieced seams can end up much shorter than a block with only two seams. Using scant ¼" seams allows for this loft (Fig. 5-3).

A good way to test for accuracy is to sew three 2"-wide strips together. Press the seams all to one side. If the unit measures exactly 5" wide, your seams are perfect! If not, try again until you've got it. This little exercise is worth it.

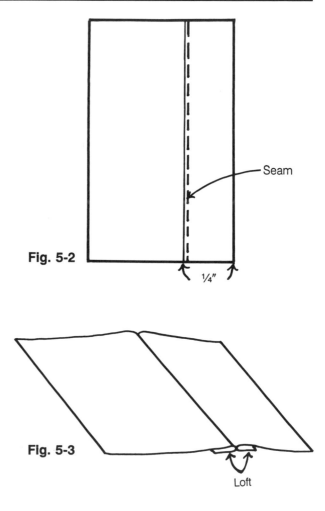

Fig. 5-2

Seam

¼"

Fig. 5-3

Loft

To Pin or Not to Pin

There are people who would refuse to sew if they had to pin. Others create metal sculptures of their seams. The majority of us use pins only at key places.

In general, a few well-placed pins help on any bias seam, set-in blocks, eight-point stars, long seams, and matched seams.

Pin across seams (Fig. 5-4), but always remove a pin before the needle comes to it. Sewing across pins is hard on your needle, weakens the seam, and shifts the fabric at that point.

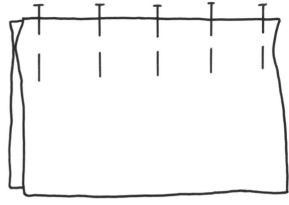

Fig. 5-4

Sewing Long Strips Together

To sew strips evenly without pinning, match up one end of the strips, sew two stitches, and stop with the needle *in* the fabric. Without stretching, match the edges of the next 12–20″. Hold tightly at this point and, pulling slightly, stitch. Stop and repeat to end of seam.

If you simply allow the two pieces to feed through without doing this, the two strips will be uneven, causing the unit to curve (Fig. 5-5).

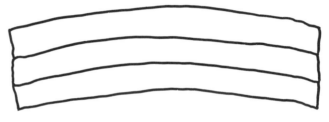

Fig. 5-5

Matching Seams

1. Always press matching seams in opposite directions (Fig. 5-6).
2. For perfect matching, pin seams together at the seam line. Stitch up to the pin before removing.
3. With practice, most seams can be matched quite nicely by butting them together with your fingers and holding them as close as possible while stitching.

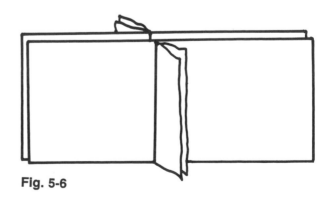

Fig. 5-6

Easing

Don't be alarmed if occasionally you need to ease two pieces together. Just pin or hold the two ends in place and *gently* pull the fabric as it is sewn. If possible, sew with the larger piece against the feed dogs. (If the two pieces simply don't fit, check to make sure you've cut them from the correct templates.) *Note:* If sewing bias to bias, never pull to ease. "Pat" them in place instead.

Set-in Pieces

1. Sew each side of the set-in piece as two separate seams.
2. Stitch each seam away from the inside corner.
3. The first seam is sewn with the set-in piece on the bottom (Fig. 5-7). The first stitch should meet the end stitch of the adjoining seam. Backstitch two or three stitches.

4. The second seam is sewn with the set-in piece on top (Fig. 5-8). The first stitch should meet the first stitch of the first seam. Backstitch two or three stitches.

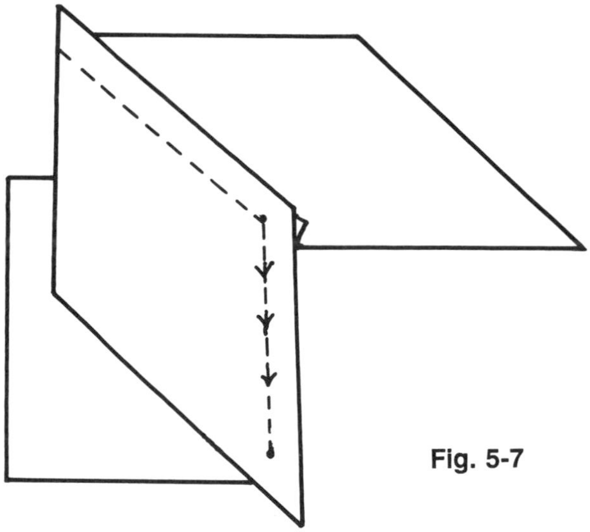

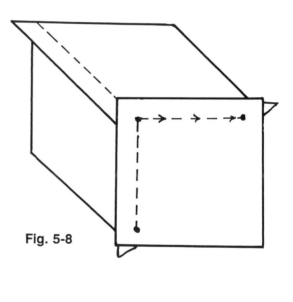

Fig. 5-8

Fig. 5-7

Joining Eight Points

1. Sew four sets of two pieces each (Fig. 5-9).
2. Press and join as shown. If sewing bias pieces (as in eight-point stars), be very careful not to stretch the seams or edges.
3. Join and press these units as shown. Trim extending corners at joining points (Fig. 5-10).
4. Insert pin straight through both pieces, at point where all seams meet (Fig. 5-11). Holding this pin straight out, pin ⅛" on either side of center point, as illustrated. Remove center pin (Fig. 5-12).
5. Starting about 2" before the center point, stitch a ¼" seam to about 2" past the center point. Be careful not to stretch the fabric. Sew over the pins slowly, gently pushing heavy thicknesses under the machine foot

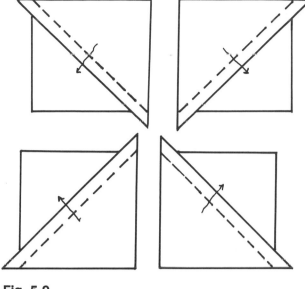

Fig. 5-9

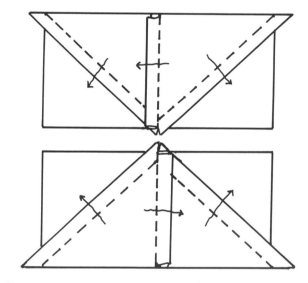

Fig. 5-10

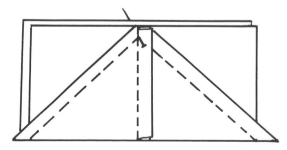

Fig. 5-11

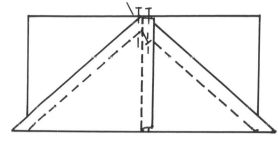

Fig. 5-12

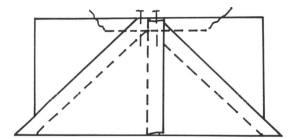

Fig. 5-13

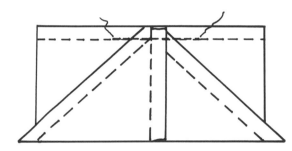

Fig. 5-14

(Fig. 5-13). (Yes, I know I said don't sew over pins, but this is an exception.)

6. Stitch entire seam, sewing on the previous 4″ of stitches (Fig. 5-14).

7. Press seam to one side. If center does not lie flat, restitch center, making a deeper seam at the center point.

Pressing

1. Never press seams open; always press to one side. Whenever possible, press the seams toward the darker fabric. *Exception:* when one seam will be matched to another, press them in opposite directions (Fig. 5-6).
2. Press with or without steam, as you prefer, from the underside. Steam can change the shape and size of a piece, so use it with caution. Use an up-and-down lifting motion.
3. Press *gently.* You are not ironing a pair of blue jeans.
4. Press on the right side, moving the iron in the same direction you're pressing the seam.

Angles and Points

After a while, you will become quite good at judging ¼″ areas. But until then, you may want to mark a few corners with ¼″ seams (remember, scant). The following are the most difficult to judge:

1. Sewing two different angles together (Fig. 5-15A).

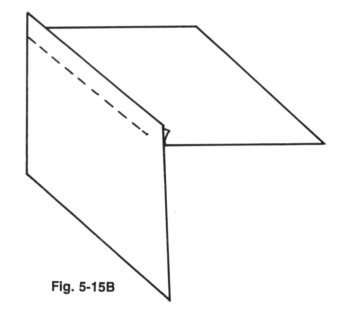

Fig. 5-15B

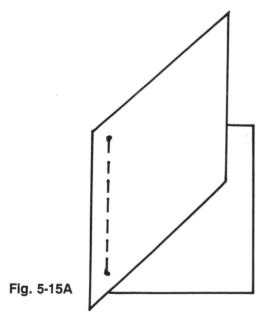

Fig. 5-15A

2. Sewing any seam that must end ¼″ from the edge, as for set-ins (Fig. 5-15B).

3. Matching two angled seams (Fig. 5-16).

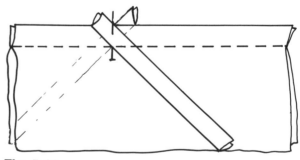

Fig. 5-16

Note: A new presser foot, called the Little Foot, has measurements to help. The foot is available from Clotilde and other mail-order sources.

Sewing Curves

1. Pin pieces at center point of seam (Fig. 5-17). Short curves can be done by sight. On longer curves, fold the pieces in half to find the centers.

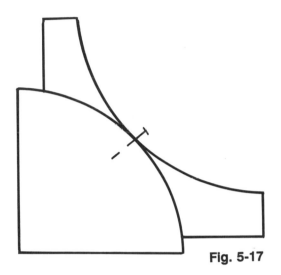

Fig. 5-17

2. With the concave (outer) curve on top, flip the pieces apart so the starting corners can be matched and held together. Pin if it helps. Take two stitches and stop with needle in fabric. Stretching as needed and lining up the raw edges, sew to center pin (Fig. 5-18).

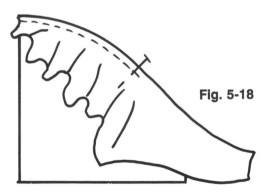

Fig. 5-18

3. With needle in fabric, flip pieces again to match corners at end of seam. Pin if needed and stitch (Fig. 5-19).

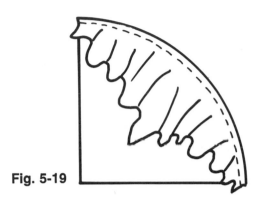

Fig. 5-19

4. Press seams to inner curve (Fig. 5-20). There is no need to clip curved seams on a quilt as the "puckery" look will be absorbed in the quilting. This is wonderful. As much as I like the Drunkard's Path, I'd never make one if I had to clip all those seams.

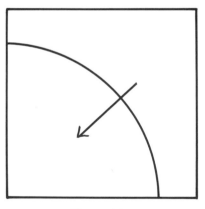

Fig. 5-20

"Factory" Method

When sewing several identical units, feed them through the machine without separating them (Fig. 5-21). This method is faster and makes it easier to keep your pieces in order. Later you can clip them apart.

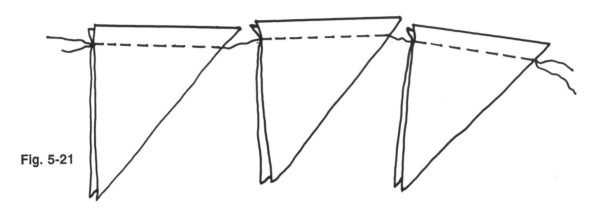

Fig. 5-21

Hand Piecing with No Marked Seam Lines

Hand piecing is becoming quite popular again, as it makes quilting a portable hobby and one that's soothing to the nerves. But drawing seam lines on the pieces is time-consuming and does terrible things to bias edges. So I devised a method of training yourself to hand piece perfect 1/4″ seams by sight.

All you do is mark the first few seams, then start making these marks lighter and lighter till you only *think* you can see them. Now try it with no marks, and you'll find you've trained your eye to "see" the 1/4″ mark. Give it a try—it really works!

Using a #10 milliner's needle (or your own favorite) and a fine quality sewing thread, sew a tiny running stitch 1/4″ from edges. Try for 16–18 stitches per inch. Evenness matters.

Carol hand piecing her Six Point Star

Sew only to the seam ends, leaving all seam allowances free. Backstitch at beginning and end of all seams (Fig. 5-22).

When moving to an adjacent seam, take the needle through seam allowances at the *exact* point where the seams meet. Continue stitching.

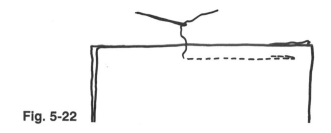

Fig. 5-22

Hand Appliqué

There are many techniques for doing hand appliqué. You may want to explore them and choose the one you prefer. The following is a simple, basic hand appliqué technique I like.

Step 1. Make a pressing template out of light-weight cardboard. I use old manila folders and index cards. Poster board and cereal boxes are good, too. (Template plastic won't work as the iron will melt it.)

Use dressmaker's carbon to trace the shape on the cardboard. Pressing templates should *not* include 1/4″ seam allowances. Do not add them.

Step 2. Cut out the appliqué shapes with a rotary cutter. Edges with an inward curve will need to be clipped at several points. Clips should be slightly *less* than 1/4″ (Fig. 5-23).

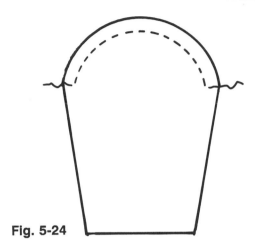

Fig. 5-24

Place the cardboard template 1/4″ from the cut edge. Gently pull the running stitch taut (Fig. 5-25). Press edges over cardboard with steam iron. Remove template. Leave the running stitch in. It can be used later, if needed, to pull the seam back in place.

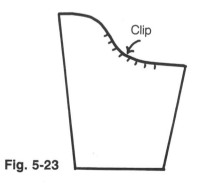

Clip

Fig. 5-23

Step 3. For shapes with curved edges, take a small running stitch 1/8″ in from the cut edge. Leave about 1″ of thread at each end (Fig. 5-24). Stitch the outer edge of each arc separately.

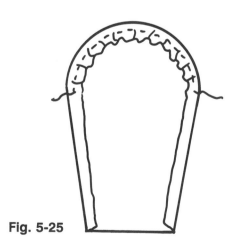

Fig. 5-25

To create sharp points, clip excess fabric to ¼″ from point. Fold down on template (Fig. 5-26). Fold points along template edge (Fig. 5-27). Fold seam allowances in. Press (Fig. 5-28).

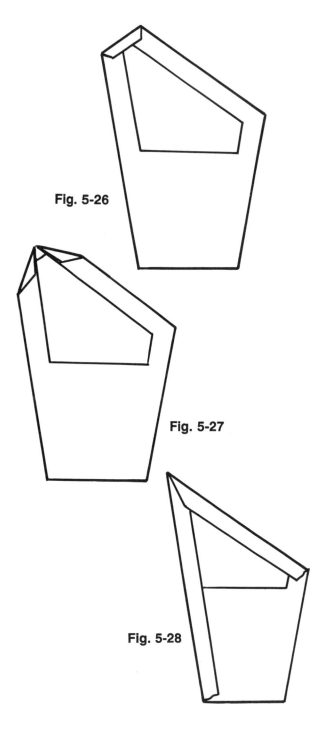

Fig. 5-26

Fig. 5-27

Fig. 5-28

Step 4. Pin or baste piece in place. For fine appliqué stitches:

- Use a #10 or #12 sharp sewing needle.

- Use fine sewing thread, either silk or silk-finish. To prevent twisting while sewing, use the thread in the direction it comes off the spool (Fig. 5-29).

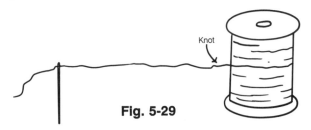

Knot

Fig. 5-29

- For almost invisible stitches, take a small stitch in the background fabric. As you come up, catch just two or three threads of the fold of the appliqué piece (Fig. 5-30).

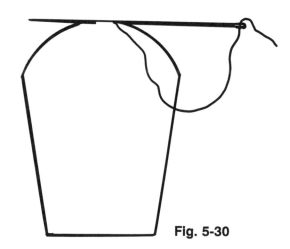

Fig. 5-30

- Start the next background stitch as close as possible to the stitch taken in the fold.

Machine "Hand Appliqué"

An easy, fast method of achieving the fine look of hand appliqué is zigzagging the edges using invisible thread (Fig. 5-31).

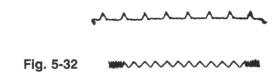

Fig. 5-32

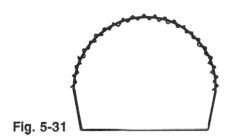

Fig. 5-31

Step 1. Set sewing machine to narrow zigzag or blind hem stitch, matching the length and width shown in Fig. 5-32.

Step 2. Lower upper tension slightly so the bobbin thread does not show on top.

Step 3. Start and stop with ½" of very tight stitches (Fig. 5-33). Stitch in a continuous unbroken line as much as possible.

½"   ½"

Fig. 5-33

Handling Bias

Next to maintaining a scant ¼" seam, handling bias is the most ignored key to easy piecing.

1. Learn what bias is and form the habit of being aware of it: *Straight grain* is the two directions (lengthwise and crosswise) of the threads used to weave the fabric. *Bias* is any other direction. *True bias* is a 45° angle to the straight grain (Fig. 5-34).

2. When sewing a bias edge to a straight edge, try to sew with the bias piece on the bottom. If it's on top, your machine foot will stretch it by pushing the fabric ahead.

3. When pressing a piece with a bias edge, either set the iron down and pick it up without moving it, or gently move the iron *with the grain* of the bias piece (Fig. 5-35).

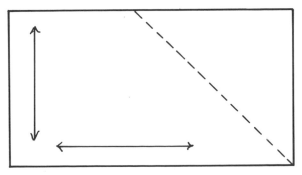

Fig. 5-34

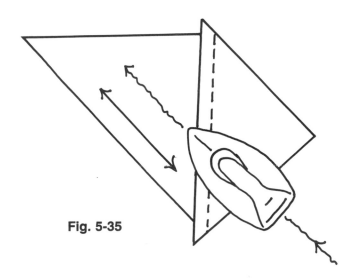

Fig. 5-35

4. If you've prewashed a fabric that will be cut up into triangles, diamonds, or other bias shapes, use a spray-on fabric sizing when ironing it.

5. As your project grows in size and weight, learn to handle it flat or folded, rather than picking it up at a raw edge. Otherwise, the weight of the quilt will stretch any unstitched bias edges.

Recognizing Grain of Fabric

There will be times when you must sew the bias edge of a shape that appears to have identical edges. Which is the bias edge?

Of course, you could easily tell which is the bias edge by stretching it, but you'd ruin the piece. Learn to "see" the threads of your fabric and you'll begin to recognize bias edges without even thinking about it.

Start by closely examining a light-colored piece of fabric. You'll see tiny lines running in two directions. You're seeing the threads that were used to weave the fabric. The direction of these threads is the straight grain. Lengthwise grain refers to the long threads first laid in the weaving loom. The threads are taut, allowing no "give."

Crosswise grain refers to the threads that are woven back and forth across the fabric. They run from selvage to selvage (the woven edge of the fabric) (Fig. 5-36). Pull in this direction and you'll feel the difference from the lengthwise grain. The fabric "gives" quite a bit!

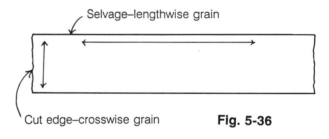

Selvage–lengthwise grain

Cut edge–crosswise grain

Fig. 5-36

Sewing the Quilt Top Blocks Together

If space allows, lay all the blocks out on the floor (or table) before sewing. Stack the first two columns in order, keeping the top block of the quilt on the top of the stack (Fig. 5-37). Sew the two top squares together (part of row 1). *Without cutting the thread,* sew the next two squares together (part of row 2). Continue in this manner till entire stack is sewn (Fig. 5-38.)

Stack column three, and, starting at the top, sew the squares to column two. Continue adding columns until all vertical seams have been completed (Fig. 5-39).

Press seams on alternating rows to the left. Press remaining seams to the right (Fig. 5-40).

Stitch horizontal seams (Fig. 5-41). Press all in same direction.

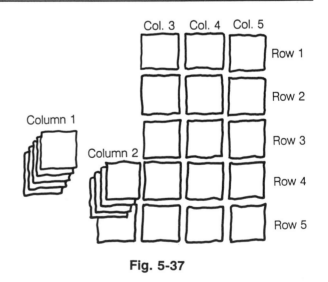

Col. 3 Col. 4 Col. 5

Row 1

Row 2

Column 1

Column 2

Row 3

Row 4

Row 5

Fig. 5-37

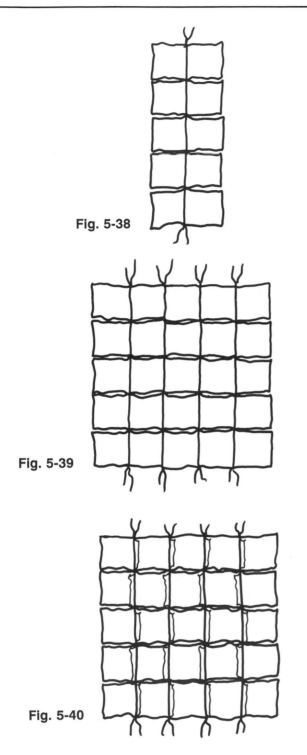

Fig. 5-38

Fig. 5-39

Fig. 5-40

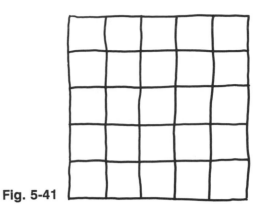

Fig. 5-41

On-Point Quilts

On-point quilts are made up of squares that are turned so the corners of the block are pointing to the top, bottom, and sides of the quilt.

This leaves triangular areas along the edges and corners that must be filled in. The easiest method is the floating version. In this, as shown in Fig. 5-42, the triangles are cut slightly larger than needed. As one row is sewn to another, the seam simply extends across this excess fabric.

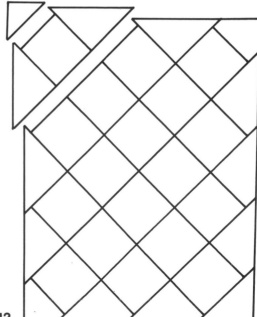

Fig. 5-42

When finished, the blocks appear to be floating on the background.

To prepare the side triangles of the quilt, cut a square in half diagonally to make two triangles. The diagonal edges will be on the bias grain. They are set into the quilt with these bias edges surrounding the quilt, which means they can be steamed and eased later if needed.

But they could also stretch while you're working. To keep from stretching this bias, I recommend the following steps:

1. Fold square in half. Press (Fig. 5-43).

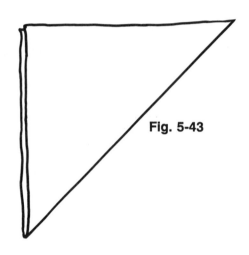

Fig. 5-43

2. Staystitch ¼" on each side of the fold (Fig. 5-44).

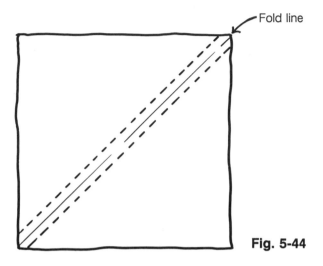

Fold line

Fig. 5-44

3. Coat lightly with spray starch. When dry, cut pieces apart (Fig. 5-45).

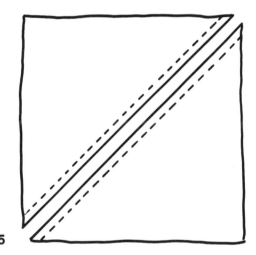

Fig. 5-45

Borders

First Border Only

Lay entire pieced center on a flat surface. Pin one piece of border fabric to side edge, right sides together. Cut second side piece the same length. Pin to second side edge. If second piece is too long, trim both pieces to same size and ease the first side to fit. Stitch (Fig. 5-46). Attach end pieces in same manner (Fig. 5-47).

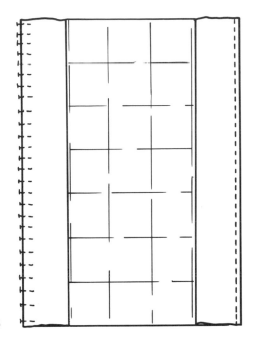

Fig. 5-46

Fig. 5-47

Remaining Borders

Remaining borders should not require measuring and pinning, but are otherwise added in the same sequence.

Mitering Borders—Speedy Method

1. Sew border strips to sides. Backstitch at beginning and end of each seam. Leave seam allowance at ends free. Place short lengthwise edge of Miterite against border seam line as shown. Draw along angled edge (seam line) (Fig. 5-48).

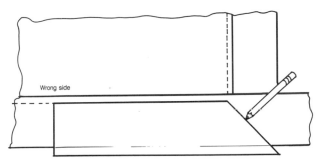

Fig. 5-48

2. Move seam line guide of Miterite over line drawn in Step 1. Draw along angled edge as shown (cutting line) (Fig. 5-49). Repeat on all corners. Sew right sides together, on seam lines (Fig. 5-50). Trim along cutting line.

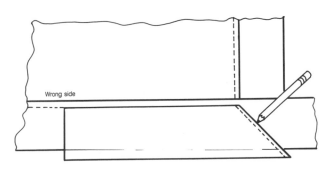

Fig. 5-49

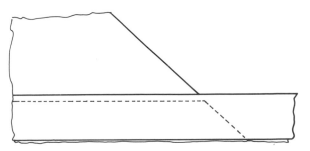

Fig. 5-50

Mitering Borders—Traditional Method

1. Sew borders to quilt, centering each strip on the quilt edge. Border strips should extend equal amounts on both ends. Stitching must stop ¼" from quilt edge end. Backstitch to secure.
2. With wrong side up, gently smooth the left border over the right one. Draw a diagonal line from the inner seam to the point where outer edges cross (Fig. 5-51).
3. Fold quilt, right sides together, till adjacent border edges are lined up with each other (Fig. 5-50). Stitch along diagonal line, stitching from outer edge to inner seam. Do not catch original border seams. Backstitch.

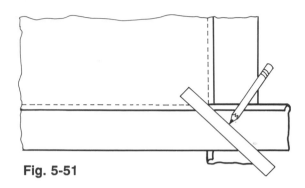

Fig. 5-51

4. Check corner shape—it should form a 90° corner. Trim seams to ½". Press open.

Marking the Quilt Top

Any marking of quilting lines should be done just before basting.

If your quilting is to follow a seam line or appliqué edge, you will not need to mark it. For designs in open areas, use a washable marker or chalk pencil. (Marks made with a lead pencil do not wash out.) Mark very lightly. This is nicer to the quilt and easier to remove.

Be sure to test any markers on a scrap of the same fabric first.

Preparing the Backing

Wash and iron backing fabric. Cut and seam as needed. Sew ¾" seams. Remove selvages. Press seams open.

The finished backing should be at least 1½–2" bigger than the top on all sides.

Basting the Quilt

You'll need a large, flat surface to work on. Mark the center of this surface and the center of your quilt backing. Matching these centers, lay the quilt backing *wrong side up* on the table. Center the batting on top of the backing. Center the quilt top, right side up, on the batting.

To be sure there are no folds or wrinkles on the bottom, pull gently on each of the four sides of the backing fabric. Repeat this every time you reposition the quilt during the basting process.

Barbara, Teresa, Lael, Sue, and Margaret pin basting the Indian Star

Starting at the center and working out, pin through all layers, using 1″ long, nickel-plated safety pins. Position pins every 3–4″ (Fig. 5-52). Avoid placing any directly on a line to be quilted.

When entire area on top of the table has been basted, carefully slide the quilt so an unbasted area is now on top. Repeat until quilt is completely basted.

Check the underside for pleats and wrinkles. You may want to rebaste an area.

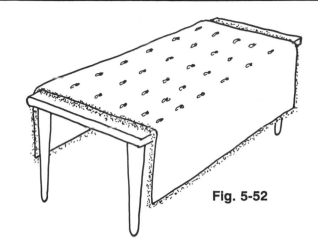

Fig. 5-52

Hand Quilting

Hand quilting is basically a running stitch holding the three layers together. You'll need quilting thread, short needles called "betweens" (#8 is easiest to learn with, but #10 will give you shorter stitches), a thimble (don't give up—you'll enjoy quilting more when you learn to use one!), and some sort of frame. Start with a small lap frame. If you do a lot of quilting, check out the various floor frames available.

The stitch requires practice. Start with a tiny knot. Enter the fabric about 1″ from the first quilting stitch. Snap the thread just hard enough to pull the knot through the top layer, catching it in the batting (Fig. 5-53).

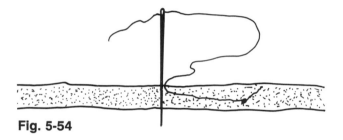

Fig. 5-54

Repeat these two motions, using your thumb (upper hand) to push the fabric over the point (Fig. 5-55).

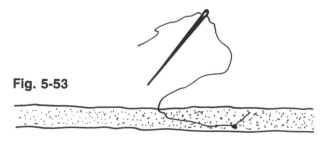

Fig. 5-53

With your free hand underneath the quilt, insert the needle straight down (Fig. 5-54). As soon as your finger feels the point, "rock" the needle down, at the same time pushing the point up.

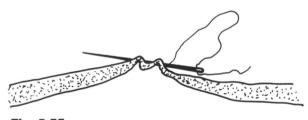

Fig. 5-55

To end the thread, take one or two tiny backstitches, then come out about 1″ away, and cut thread short, leaving a 1″ tail end anchored in the batting.

With today's bonded batting, it is not as important to get tiny stitches. Try first to get *even* stitches, then try for shorter ones if you wish.

Hints for Machine Quilting

Machine quilting is even easier today because of the walking foot (or even-feed foot) and transparent thread.

🔖 When quilting over two or more colors of fabric, use a clear thread on the top. You'll need to loosen the top tension to get a perfect stitch. For the bobbin, choose a good sewing thread to match the backing fabric.

🔖 With a walking foot, you will not have to push or pull the quilt through the machine. Be careful, however, that the weight of the quilt does not create a drag.

🔖 Where to quilt is personal. Most people pick out specific seam lines and follow them. Your movement is limited when you are machine quilting a large item, so you'll need to choose your quilting lines with this in mind. There are attachments available, however, that allow a free movement of the fabric while stitching. You may want to experiment with these. (See the Bibliography for a good book on machine quilting.)

🔖 For machine quilting, use a longer stitch—6–8 stitches per inch—it feeds through easier and has a puffier look. If you're using a clear thread on top, loosen your upper tension to prevent the thread from breaking.

Susan machine quilting All Tied Up

🔖 The trick to machine quilting is to learn how to handle bulk. Roll each side tightly toward the center quilting line. Bicycle clips help keep these two rolls in place (Fig. 5-56). Fold as shown to make a manageable bundle to put in your lap (Fig. 5-57). Using a walking foot and a long machine stitch, sew the entire length of this quilting line. Reroll the quilt to the next area and stitch. Repeat till quilt is done.

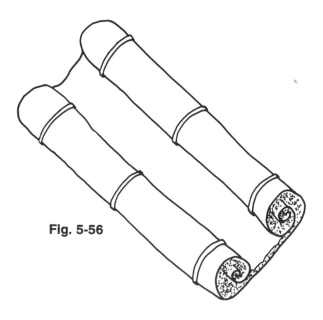

Fig. 5-56

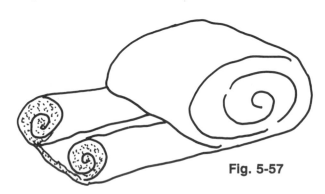

Fig. 5-57

Tying a Quilt

This is the fastest way to finish a quilt. Follow the same procedure for basting, but instead of pinning, tie it.

I use #3 pearl cotton, double strand, and a large darning needle. You'll need pliers or a piece of rubber to pull the needle through. Using a long piece of thread (about 36″ when doubled), take one stitch through all layers (Fig. 5-58). Knot this by tying it just twice (Fig. 5-59).

You'll gather the quilt at the tied spot, but don't worry, it'll work out as it's used. Cut the tail ends 1″ long and go on to the next one.

In a tied quilt, you must use either bonded batting or flannel fabric.

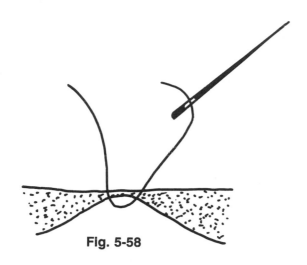

Fig. 5-58

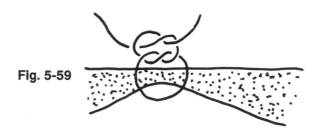

Fig. 5-59

Binding the Edges

Binding Straight Edges

Binding the edges is the last step in creating a quilt. The quickest way is to turn the raw edge of the outer border to the back and stitch it in place. To do this the outer border must be cut 1³⁄₄″ wider than the finished width, allowing 1¹⁄₂″ for turnback. (All outer borders in this book include that extra width.)

1. With right sides up, trim off excess batting and backing so all edges are even with outer border edge (Fig. 5-60).
2. With back sides of quilt up, trim 1″ off backing and batting (Fig. 5-61). *(Do not cut off any border fabric.)*
3. Turn 1¹⁄₂″ of border to the back of the quilt. You will be turning back ¹⁄₂″ of the batting/ backing also. This is necessary to retain a plump binding when quilt is used. Turn under ¹⁄₂″ of raw edge. Pin. Machine stitch.

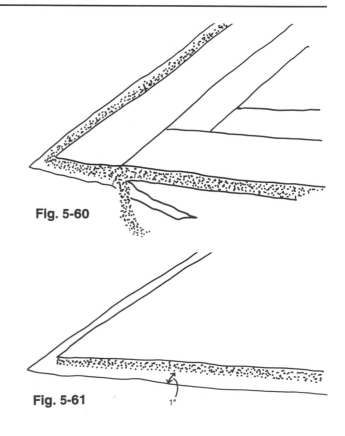

Fig. 5-60

Fig. 5-61

4. For easy mitered corners, fold corner wrong side out, as shown (Fig. 5-62). Measure 2⅛″ from point. Mark or pin.

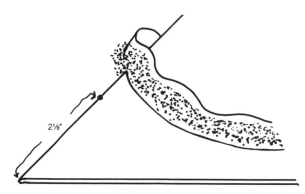

Fig. 5-62

5. Fold point at mark, keeping cut edges together. Mark quilt at fold line (Fig. 5-63). Stitch 1½″ from fold. Backstitch. Trim seam to ½″, tapering at corner (Fig. 5-64). Turn to right side. Mitered corner will fall neatly in place, leaving ½″ free to turn under (Fig. 5-65).

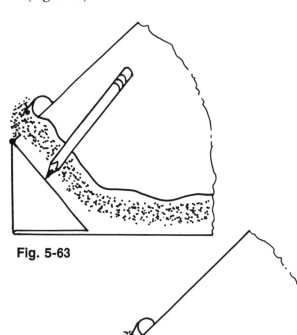

Fig. 5-63

Fig. 5-64

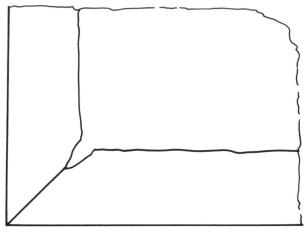

Fig. 5-65

6. Turn ½″ under. Pin in place. Topstitch (Fig. 5-66).

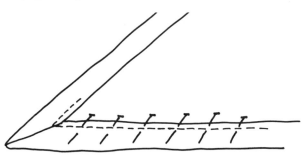

Fig. 5-66

Binding Curved or Shaped Edges

1. Trim backing and batting even with quilt top.
2. Cut bias strips 2¼″ wide. Sew end to end (Fig. 5-67).

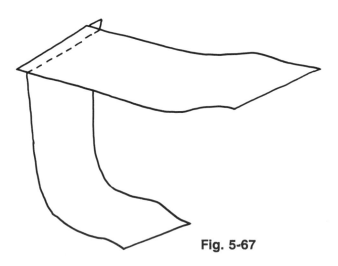

Fig. 5-67

3. Fold strip in half lengthwise, wrong sides together (Fig. 5-68). Press.

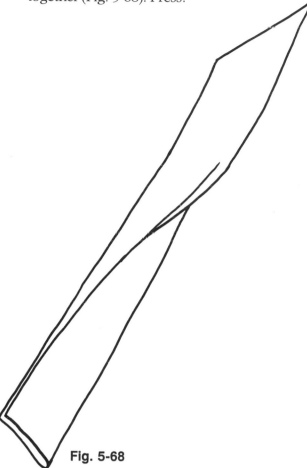

Fig. 5-68

Inside Corners. Stitch ³/₈″ into corner, lift presser foot to pivot, continue (Fig. 5-70). When bias is turned to back, make a tiny fold with the excess (Fig. 5-71).

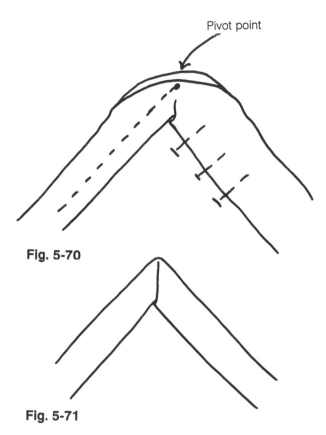

Fig. 5-70

Fig. 5-71

4. Pinning both edges of strip to top edge of quilt, stitch strip to quilt, using ³/₈″ seam. Begin along a side, not at a corner. Leave a 6″ piece of the strip unstitched (Fig. 5-69). Pin every 6″ along long, curved edges to be sure bias is not being stretched. Pin at corners.

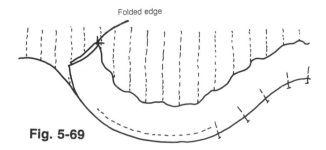

Folded edge

Fig. 5-69

Outer Corners. Stop stitching ³/₈″ before corner, back tack 1–2 stitches, cut threads. Lift presser foot, fold bias strip as shown (Fig. 5-72). Fold should be even with raw edge. Begin stitching again at fold (Fig. 5-73). When turned to the back, bias will form a neatly mitered corner:

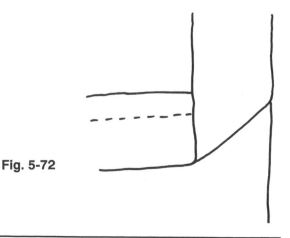

Fig. 5-72

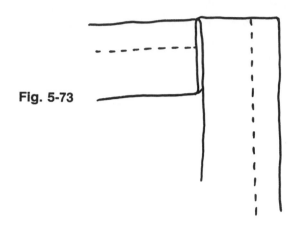

Fig. 5-73

5. Turn bias to back of quilt. Hand stitch folded edge to quilt, covering machine stitching. Use same stitch as for hand appliqué.

Caring for Your Quilt

Machine Washing and Drying

Machine washing and drying work fine provided you have used a bonded batting and have a washer and dryer large enough to accommodate your quilt. Use the gentlest cycle and a mild detergent. Use your dryer on delicate cycle only. *Never* use a hot dryer. Dry only to a slightly damp stage. Remove quilt and finish the drying process flat on a blanket or bed.

Hand Washing and Drying

Fill the bathtub half full of lukewarm water. Use a mild detergent. Squeeze gently and swish the quilt around in the water, but never lift it while it is wet. The weight of the wet quilt at the bottom will snap the quilting threads. Rinse several times. Squeeze as much moisture from the quilt as possible. *Do not lift or wring.* When transporting a wet quilt, fold it into a bundle and carry it in your arms. Dry your quilt on a blanket spread out on a large flat surface, such as the floor in a spare bedroom. Outside on a sunny day works well, but be sure to put the top side of your quilt down to prevent fading.

Storage

Fold your quilt loosely and wrap it in a sheet or pillowcase. Never store it in plastic. Air must circulate around the quilt to preserve it.

Double Wedding Ring (Quilt 19). Sandy Lawrence. Blue, rose, and cream, 62" × 72".

Bow Tie (Quilt 3). Sue Miller. Wine and blue, 68″ × 104″.

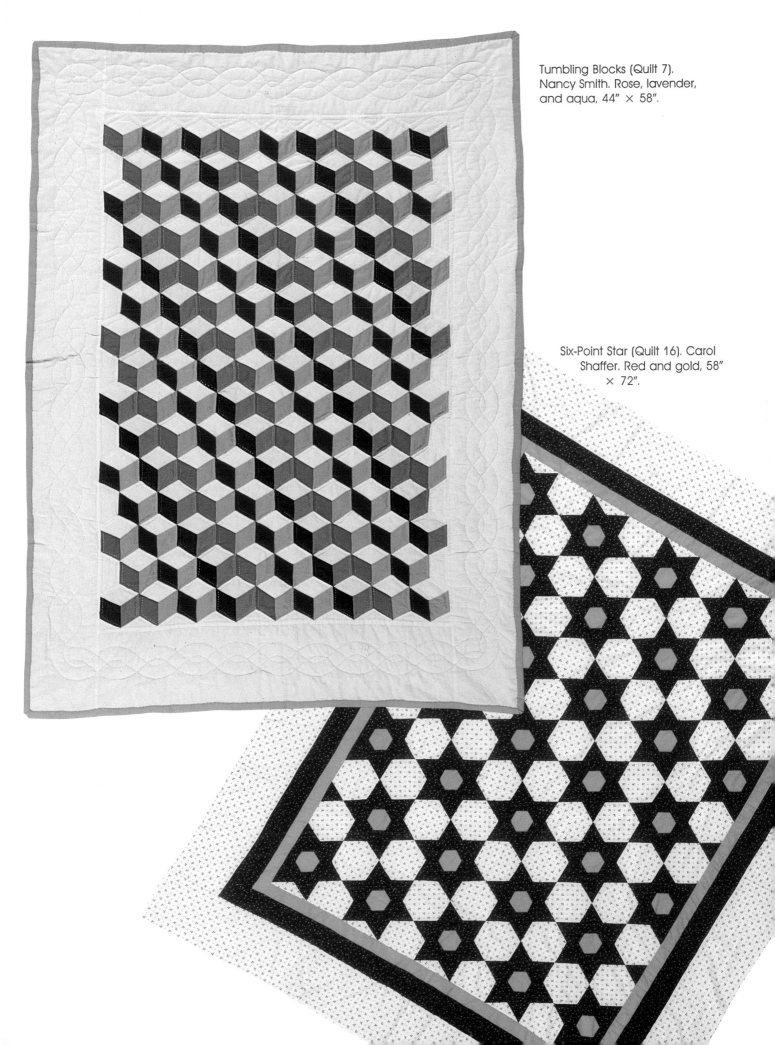

Tumbling Blocks (Quilt 7). Nancy Smith. Rose, lavender, and aqua, 44″ × 58″.

Six-Point Star (Quilt 16). Carol Shaffer. Red and gold, 58″ × 72″.

Whirling Cones (Quilt 17). Lael Alpiger. Primary colors, 50" × 60".

Double Wedding Ring (Quilt 19). Julie Beck. Primary colors, 41" × 52".

Drunkard's Path (Quilt 10). Donna Poster. Red and white, 48″ × 60″.

Grandmother's Flower Garden (Quilt 1). Kathy Lang. Pink and teal, 106″ × 103″.

All Tied Up (Quilt 9). Sue Saiter. Peach and green, 48″ × 60″.

Fan (Quilt 6). Margaret Parks. Soft pink and aqua, 90" × 104".

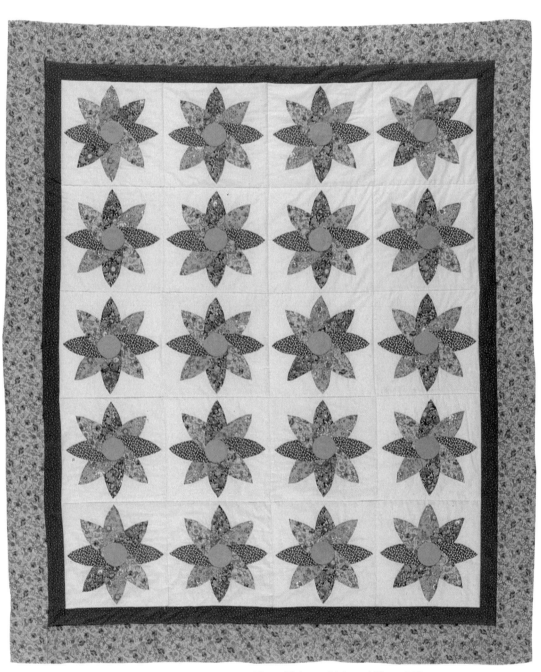

Little Dahlia (Quilt 4). Teresa Kline. Pink and blue, 60″ × 72″.

20 QUILTS

Now for the fun part. Making a real quilt!

I assume you've practiced my Speedy System enough to understand the basic principles. Well, good—you do need to do that. But learning to quilt is really like learning to play the piano. Practicing the scales is necessary, but the real fun comes when you get to play the songs.

So, as a kind of bonus, I've included twenty quilts to get you going. Some are old favorites, some are new, but they've all been tested in my classes and they're all fun!

A few explanations about this quilt section:

1. The abbreviations are CR (crib), TW (twin), D (double), Q (queen), K (king), SQ (square), and OB (oblong).
2. The bedspread sizes (TW–K) include a 12–14″ drop to cover the top of a dust ruffle. They are all long enough to go over a pillow and tuck under it. The square and oblong sizes make nice tablecloths, wall hangings, lap throws, or children's blankets.
3. For clarity, I have tried to keep my instructions simple. If you need further help on any sewing technique, look in Chapter 5, Basic Construction Techniques.

I've divided the quilts into three categories:

Susan and Sue S. quilt while Lael and Ferbie watch

Beginner

1. Grandmother's Flower Garden
2. Dresden Plate
3. Bow Tie
4. Little Dahlia
5. Texas Trellis
6. Fan
7. Tumbling Blocks

12. Always Friends
13. Peacock
14. Magnolias
15. Clamshell
16. Six-Point Star
17. Whirling Cones

Intermediate

8. Indian Star
9. All Tied Up
10. Drunkard's Path
11. Nighttime

Advanced

18. Flower Basket
19. Double Wedding Ring
20. Nosegay

1. GRANDMOTHER'S FLOWER GARDEN
Beginner

Dimensions (Inches)

	CR	TW	D	Q	K	SQ	OB
Finished Quilt	41 × 57	67 × 103	80 × 103	93 × 103	106 × 103	54 × 57	54 × 80

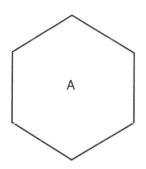

To Speed-Cut:
A. Hexagon

Cutting Instructions

	CR	TW	D	Q	K	SQ	OB
Number needed							
Center (fabric 1)	17	49	58	67	76	22	31
1st ring (fabric 2)	94	278	332	386	440	120	174
2nd ring (fabric 3)	184	548	656	764	872	244	342
Connectors (fabric 4)	150	410	488	566	644	196	264
Binding	Cut bias strips 2½" wide						

General Information

	CR	TW	D	Q	K	SQ	OB
Rings across	3	5	6	7	8	4	4
Rings down	5	9	9	9	9	5	7
Total	13	41	50	59	68	18	25
Total half-rings	4	8	8	8	8	6	6

Grandmother's Flower Garden Instructions

Note: *This is one of the few quilts that actually takes longer to machine-piece than to hand-piece. Believe me—I tried it! Try my method for hand-piecing with no marked seam lines (see Chapter 5)—it's easy and fun.*

Piecing

A. Piecing basic units:

Step 1. Join flower pieces in rows (Fig. 1).

Step 2. Join these rows (Fig. 2).

B. Joining units:

Step 1. Sew two connecting pieces between flower units (Fig. 3).

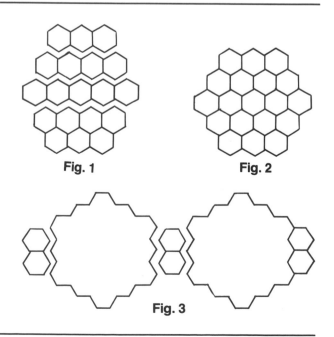

Fig. 1

Fig. 2

Fig. 3

Step 2. Join connecting pieces to form horizontal rows (Fig. 4).

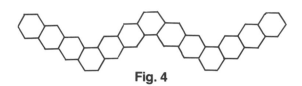

Fig. 4

Step 3. Join flower rows and connecting rows (Fig. 5).

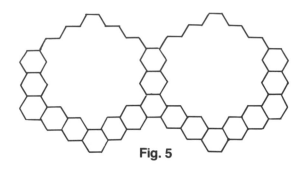

Fig. 5

Finishing

A. Quilt as desired.
B. Cut bias binding 2½″ wide. Bind, following "stepped" edges.

Yardages

Fabrics	CR	TW	D	Q	K	SQ	OB
Fabric 1 (center)	¼	½	⅝	¾	¾	¼	⅜
Fabric 2 (1st ring)	1	2¼	2⅞	3¼	3⅝	1⅛	1½
Fabric 3 (2nd ring)	1½	4½	5½	6¼	7⅛	2⅛	3
Fabric 4 (connecting rings)	1½	3½	4	4½	5¼	1¾	2¼
Backing	1¾	6	6	8¼	9¼	3¼	3¾
Bias Binding	¾	1¼	1½	1½	1¾	¾	1

Yardage Notes

• All yardages include a small amount for shrinkage and waste.

Options

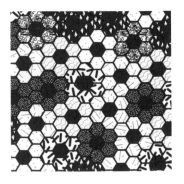

Grandmother's Flower Garden
Design Page

For quick reference or design-your own:

1. Copy this page.
2. Trim copy to desired quilt size.
3. Color design.

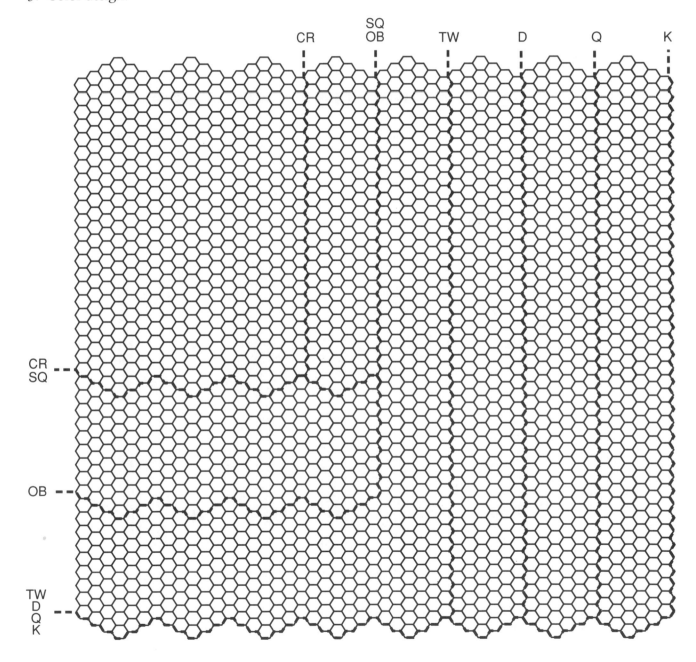

2. DRESDEN PLATE
Beginner

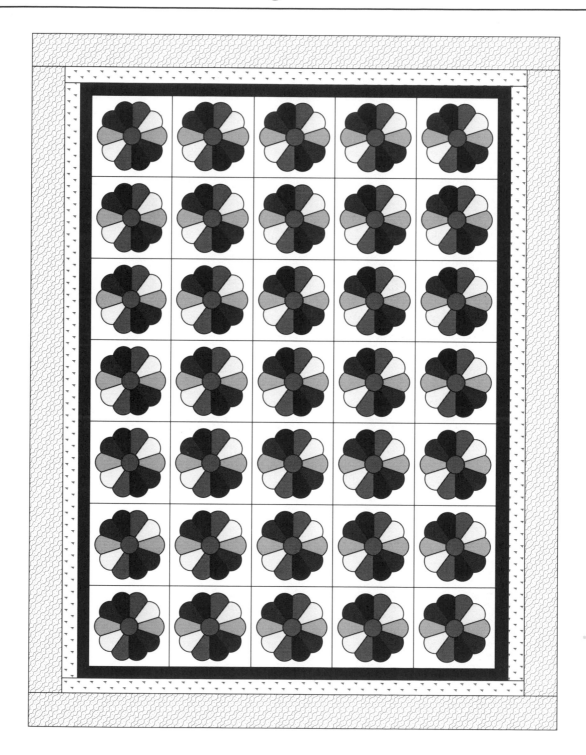

Dimensions (Inches)

	CR	TW	D	Q	K	SQ	OB
Finished Quilt	46 × 58	70 × 106	82 × 106	92 × 104	108 × 108	64 × 64	60 × 72
Center	36 × 48	60 × 96	60 × 84	72 × 84	84 × 84	48 × 48	48 × 60
1st border	1½	1½	1½	1½	1½	1½	1½
2nd border	3½	3½	3	3	3	2½	4½
3rd border	—	—	6½	5½	7½	4	—

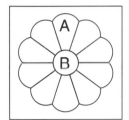

To Speed-Cut:
    A. Cone, arc end
    B. Circle, 4″

Cutting Instructions

	CR	TW	D	Q	K	SQ	OB
Number needed							
A (fabrics 1 thru 5, each)	24	80	70	84	98	32	40
B (fabric 6)	12	40	35	42	49	16	20
Background blocks (fabric 7)	12	40	35	42	49	16	20
Cut widths							
Cut 1st border	2″	2″	2″	2″	2″	2″	2″
Cut 2nd border	5½″	5½″	3½″	3½″	3½″	3″	6½″
Cut 3rd border	—	—	8½″	7½″	9½″	6″	—

General Information

	CR	TW	D	Q	K	SQ	OB
Blocks Across	3	5	5	6	7	4	4
Blocks Down	4	8	7	7	7	4	5
Total	12	40	35	42	49	16	20

Dresden Plate
Instructions

Piecing

A. Piecing blocks:

Step 1. Join cone pieces, factory method. Do NOT backstitch (Fig. 1).

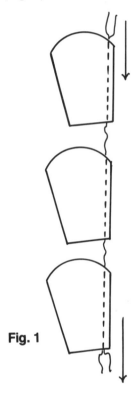

Fig. 1

Step 2. Using the eye end of a needle, pull out about 1/2″ of the seam at the wide end of the cones. Do NOT clip threads. (Fig. 2).

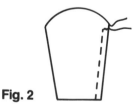

Fig. 2

Step 3. With running stitch and pressing templates, prepare circles and outer edges of cones for appliqué (Fig. 3).

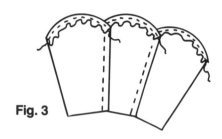

Fig. 3

Note: *Seam allowances will be wider than 1/4″ at ends of arcs (Fig. 4).*

Fig. 4

Step 4. Hand or machine appliqué circles to plates (Fig. 5).

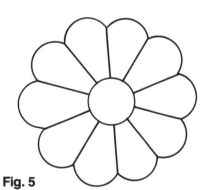

Fig. 5

Step 5. Appliqué plates to background squares (Fig. 6).

Fig. 6

B. Join blocks.

C. Add borders.

Finishing

A. Quilt as desired.

B. Turn 1½″ of outer border to back of quilt. Turn under ½″. Pin and stitch.

Yardages

Fabrics	CR	TW	D	Q	K	SQ	OB
1 thru 5, each (A)	½	1½	1¼	1½	1¾	¾	¾
6 (B)	⅜	¾	¾	⅞	⅞	⅜	⅜
7 (Background blocks)	1½	5	4½	5	6	2½	2½
1st border	½	¾	¾	¾	¾	¾	½
2nd border	1¼	1½	1¼	1¼	1½	1	1½
3rd border	—	—	2½	2¼	3½	1½	—
Backing	3	6½	8¼	8½	10	4	4

Cutting Borders

• To cut length of outer borders, add 6″ to finished sizes of quilt.

• Cut all other borders to finished quilt size.

• Trim as needed.

• All outer borders include 1½″ extra to turn back for finished edge.

Yardage Notes

• All yardages include a small amount for shrinkage and waste.

• Yardages are for pieced borders, to conserve fabric. You may prefer an unpieced border, especially on wider borders. Use the longest side of your finished quilt to determine how many yards to buy.

Options

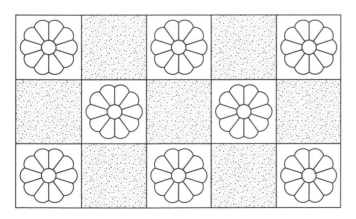

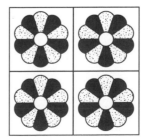

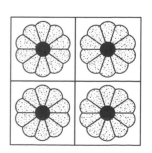

Dresden Plate
Design Page

For quick reference or design-your-own:

1. Copy this page.
2. Trim copy to desired quilt size.
3. Color design.

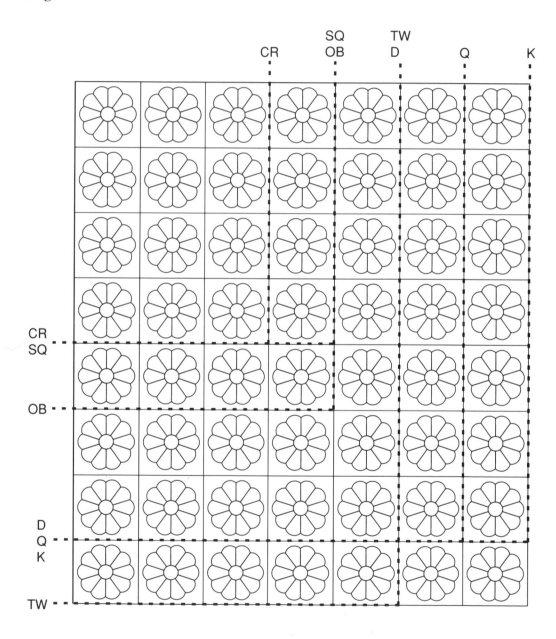

3. BOW TIE
Beginner

Dimensions (Inches)

	CR	TW	D	Q	K	SQ	OB
Finished Quilt	48 × 60	70 × 106	84 × 108	86 × 110	108 × 108	64 × 64	60 × 72
Center	36 × 48	48 × 84	60 × 84	60 × 84	84 × 84	48 × 48	48 × 60
1st border	1½	1½	1½	1½	1½	1½	1½
2nd border	4½	2½	2½	3	2½	6½	4½
3rd border	—	7	8	8½	8	—	—

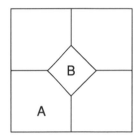

To Speed-Cut:
  A. Lop-eared Square
  B. Square

Cutting Instructions

	CR	TW	D	Q	K	SQ	OB
Number needed							
A (fabrics 1 and 2, each)	48	112	140	140	196	64	80
A (fabric 3)	96	224	280	280	392	128	160
B (fabrics 4 and 5, each)	48	112	140	140	196	64	80
Cut Widths							
Cut 1st border	2″	2″	2″	2″	2″	2″	2″
Cut 2nd border	6½″	3″	3″	3½″	3″	8½″	6½″
Cut 3rd border	—	9″	10″	10½″	10″	—	—

General Information

	CR	TW	D	Q	K	SQ	OB
Blocks Across	6	8	10	10	14	8	8
Blocks Down	8	14	14	14	14	8	10
Total	48	112	140	140	196	64	80

Bow Tie
Instructions

Piecing

A. Piecing basic units:

Step 1. Center A piece on B piece (Fig. 1). With B on top, stitch, stopping 1/4″ from each edge of B (Fig. 2).

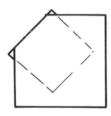 

Fig. 1   **Fig. 2**

Step 2. Repeat step 1 on opposite side of B piece (Fig. 3).

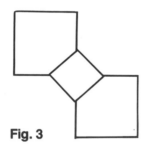

Fig. 3

Step 3. With B on top, add remaining A pieces (Fig. 4).

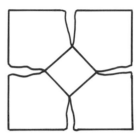

Fig. 4

Step 4. Join A pieces (Fig. 5).

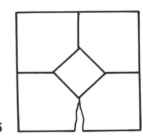

Fig. 5

B. Join units.
C. Add borders.

Finishing

A. Quilt as desired.
B. Turn 1 1/2″ of outer border to back of quilt. Turn under 1/2″. Pin and stitch.

Yardages

Fabrics	CR	TW	D	Q	K	SQ	OB
1 (A, bow 1)	3/4	1 1/4	1 1/2	1 1/2	2	3/4	1
2 (A, bow 2)	3/4	1 1/4	1 1/2	1 1/2	2	3/4	1
3 (A, background)	1 1/4	2 1/4	2 3/4	2 3/4	3 3/4	1 1/2	1 3/4
4 (B, knot 1)	1/4	5/8	3/4	3/4	1	3/8	1/2
5 (B, knot 2)	1/4	5/8	3/4	3/4	1	3/8	1/2
1st border	1/2	1/2	3/4	3/4	7/8	1/2	1/2
2nd border	1 1/2	1	1 1/8	1 1/3	1 1/4	1 3/4	1 1/2
3rd border	—	2 1/8	2 1/2	3	2 3/4	—	—
Backing	3	6 1/4	8	8 1/4	9 3/4	4	3 3/4

Cutting Borders

- To cut length of outer borders, add 6″ to finished sizes of quilt.
- Cut all other borders to finished quilt size.
- Trim as needed.
- All outer borders include 1 1/2″ extra to turn back for finished edge.

Yardage Notes

- All yardages include a small amount for shrinkage and waste.
- Yardages are for pieced borders, to conserve fabric. You may prefer an unpieced border, especially on wider borders. Use the longest side of your finished quilt to determine how many yards to buy.

Options

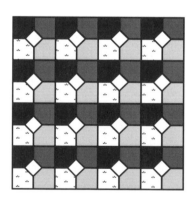

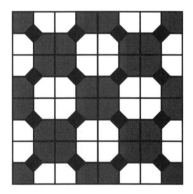

Bow Tie
Design Page

For quick reference or design-your-own:

1. Copy this page.
2. Trim copy to desired quilt size.
3. Color design.

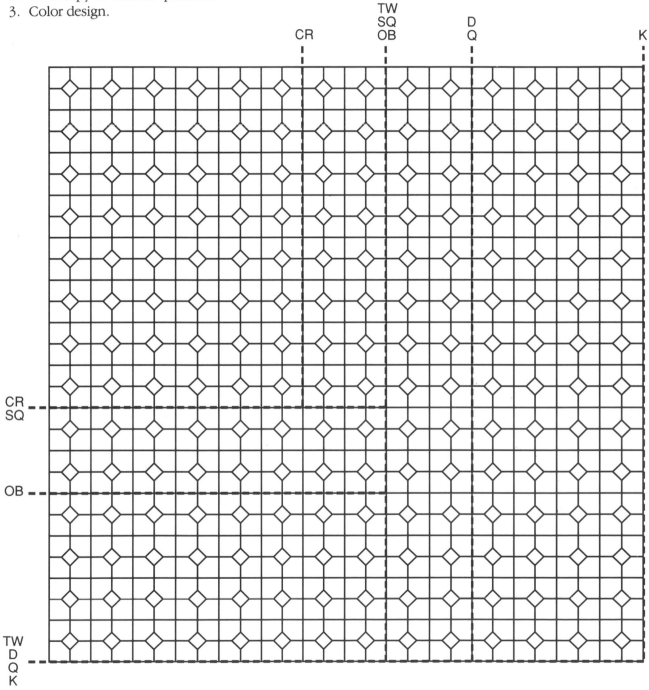

4. LITTLE DAHLIA
Beginner

Dimensions (inches)

	CR	TW	D	Q	K	SQ	OB
Finished Quilt	48 × 60	70 × 106	84 × 108	86 × 110	108 × 108	64 × 64	60 × 72
Center	36 × 48	48 × 84	60 × 84	60 × 84	84 × 84	48 × 48	48 × 60
1st border	2	1½	1½	1½	1½	1½	2
2nd border	4	3	3	4	3	2½	4
3rd border	—	1½	1½	1½	1½	4	—
4th border	—	5	6	6	6	—	—

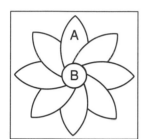

To Speed-Cut:
A. Petal
B. Circle, 3″

Cutting Instructions

	CR	TW	D	Q	K	SQ	OB
Number needed							
Background square (fabric 1)	12	28	35	35	49	16	20
B (fabric 2)	12	28	35	35	49	16	20
A (fabrics 3 thru 6, each)	24	56	70	70	98	32	40
Cut widths							
1st border	2½	2″	2″	2″	2″	2″	2½″
2nd border	6″	3½″	3½″	4½″	3½″	3″	6″
3rd border	—	2″	2″	2″	2″	6″	—
4th border	—	7″	8″	8″	8″	—	—

General Information

	CR	TW	D	Q	K	SQ	OB
Blocks Across	3	4	5	5	7	4	4
Blocks Down	4	7	7	7	7	4	5
Total	12	28	35	35	49	16	20

Little Dahlia
Instructions

Piecing

A. Piecing blocks:

Step 1. Using a running stitch and a pressing template, prepare all A and B pieces for appliqué (Fig. 1).

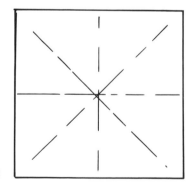

Fig. 1

Note: *When pressing petals, match bottom edges of pressing template and fabric.*

Step 2. Press background fabric lightly into eighths (Fig. 2).

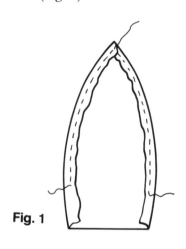

Fig. 2

Step 3. Fold each petal to find center of base edge.

Step 4. Pin each petal, matching center of petal base to center of block. Place petal point on a pressing line (Fig. 3). Overlap petals. Tuck last one under first one (Fig. 4).

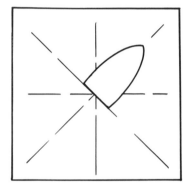

Fig. 3

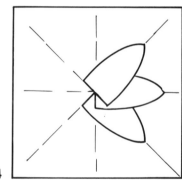

Fig. 4

Note: *Before stitching, test center circle to be sure it covers all petal edges. Reposition petals if necessary.*

Step 5. Hand or machine appliqué petal edges.

Step 6. Pin circle on center. Appliqué.

B. Sew squares together.
C. Add borders.

Finishing

A. Quilt as desired.
B. Turn 1½" of outer border to back of quilt. Turn under ½". Pin and stitch.

Yardages

Fabrics	CR	TW	D	Q	K	SQ	OB
1 (background)	1¹/₂	3³/₄	4¹/₂	4¹/₂	6	2¹/₂	2¹/₂
2 (circle B)	¹/₈	¹/₄	³/₈	³/₈	¹/₂	¹/₄	¹/₄
3 thru 6, each (petals A)	¹/₂	⁷/₈	1	1	1¹/₂	⁵/₈	⁵/₈
1st border	³/₄	³/₄	³/₄	³/₄	³/₄	³/₄	³/₄
2nd border	1¹/₂	1	1¹/₄	1¹/₂	1¹/₂	1	1¹/₂
3rd border	—	³/₄	³/₄	³/₄	³/₄	1¹/₂	—
4th border	—	2	2¹/₂	2¹/₂	3	—	—
Backing	3¹/₄	6³/₄	8¹/₂	8¹/₂	10¹/₄	4	3³/₄

Cutting Borders

- To cut length of outer borders, add 6″ to finished sizes of quilt.
- Cut all other borders to finished quilt size.
- Trim as needed.
- All outer borders include 1¹/₂″ extra to turn back for finished edge.

Yardage Notes

- All yardages include a small amount for shrinkage and waste.
- Yardages are for pieced borders, to conserve fabric. You may prefer an unpieced border, especially on wider borders. Use the longest side of your finished quilt to determine how many yards to buy.

Options

Little Dahlia
Design Page

For quick reference or design-your-own:

1. Copy this page.
2. Trim copy to desired quilt size.
3. Color design.

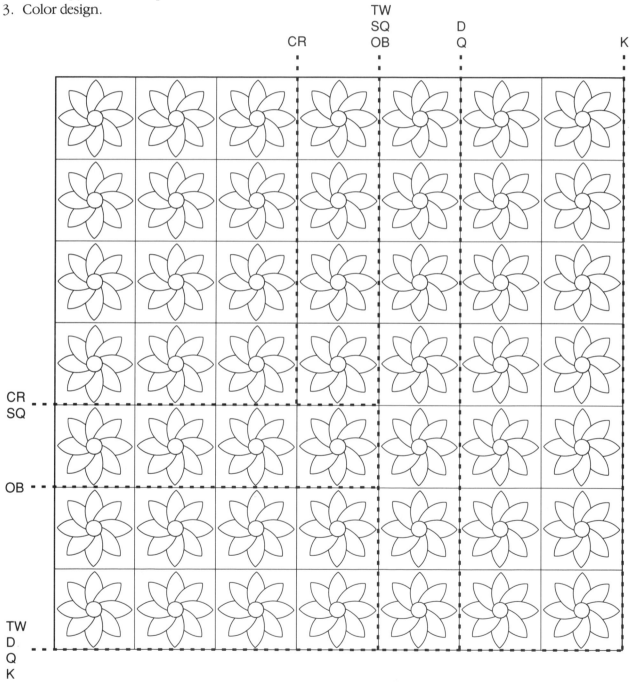

5. TEXAS TRELLIS
Beginner

Dimensions (Inches)

	CR	TW	D	Q	K	SQ	OB
Finished Quilt	42 × 56	70 × 104	84 × 104	91 × 104	105 × 104	70 × 68	56 × 80

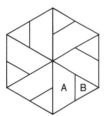

To Speed-Cut:
A. Anvil, 60°
B. Triangle, 60°

Cutting Instructions

	CR	TW	D	Q	K	SQ	OB
Number needed							
B (fabric 1)	324	1020	1224	1326	1530	660	624
A (fabric 2)	108	330	408	432	510	216	216
A (fabric 3)	108	330	408	432	510	216	192
A (fabric 4)	108	360	408	462	510	234	216
Binding			Cut bias strip 2½" wide				

General Information

	CR	TW	D	Q	K	SQ	OB
Units Across	6	10	12	13	15	10	8
Units Down (rows)	9	17	17	17	17	11	13
Total	54	170	204	221	255	110	104

Texas Trellis Instructions

Cutting Note: *If speed-cutting, all strips used for piece B must be cut on lengthwise grain.*

Piecing

A. Piecing basic units:

Step 1. Join A and B pieces (Fig. 1).

Fig. 1

Step 2. Join units to form half hexagons (Fig. 2).

B. Joining units:

Note: *It helps here to copy the basic plan, color the units, and number the strips.*

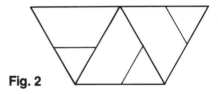

Fig. 2

Step 1. Join units to form strips (Fig. 3).

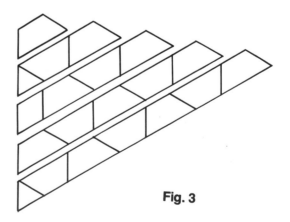

Fig. 3

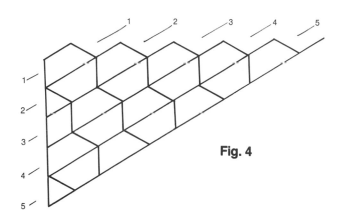

Step 2. Join strips (Fig. 4).

Finishing

A. Quilt as desired.
B. Cut bias binding 2½″ wide. Bind, following "stepped" edges.

Fig. 4

Yardages

Fabrics	CR	TW	D	Q	K	SQ	OB
1 (B, background)	1¼	3½	4¼	4½	5¼	2¼	2¼
2 (A)	1	2¼	2¾	3	3½	1½	1⅝
3 (A)	1	2¼	2¾	3	3½	1½	1½
4 (A)	1	2½	2¾	3¼	3½	1¾	1⅝
Binding	¾	1¼	1½	1½	1¾	1	1
Backing	3	6½	7¾	8½	10¼	4¼	3¾

Yardage Notes

• All yardages include a small amount for shrinkage and waste.

Options

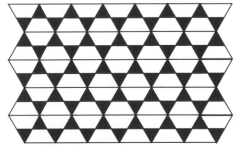

Texas Trellis
Design Page

For quick reference or design-your-own:

1. Copy this page.
2. Trim copy to desired quilt size.
3. Color design.

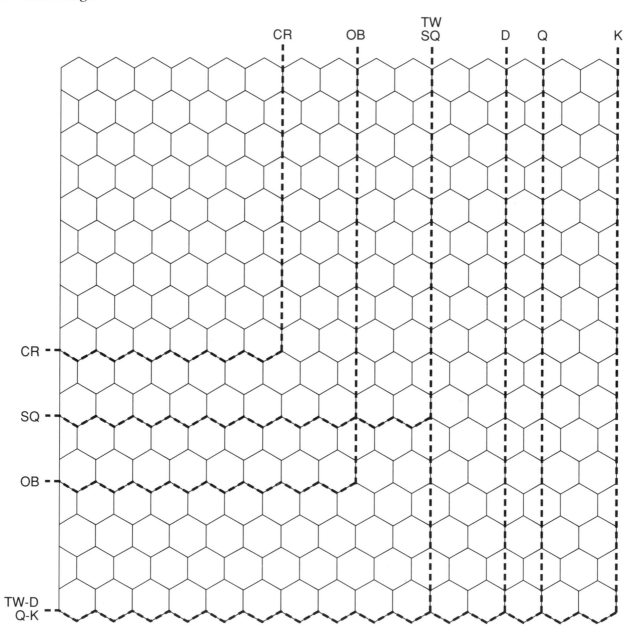

6. FAN
Beginner

Dimensions (Inches)

	CR	TW	D	Q	K	SQ	OB
Finished Quilt	46 × 64	76 × 104	90 × 104	92 × 106	110 × 110	66 × 66	59 × 73
Center	40 × 58	58 × 86	72 × 86	72 × 86	86 × 86	58 × 58	43 × 57
1st border	3	1½	1½	1½	1½	1	1½
2nd border	—	3	3	3	3	3	2½
3rd border	—	4½	4½	5½	1½	—	4
4th border	—	—	—	—	6	—	—

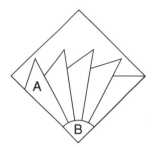

To Speed-Cut:
   A. Cone, point end
   B. Fan

Cut background blocks: $10^{1}/_{2}$ × $10^{1}/_{2}$

Cut squares for:
   Edge triangles: 12″ × 12″
   Corner triangles: 9″ × 9″

Cutting Instructions

	CR	TW	D	Q	K	SQ	OB
Number needed							
Background squares (fabric 7) and B (fabric 1)	18	39	50	50	61	25	18
A (Fabrics 2 thru 6, each)	18	39	50	50	61	25	18
Edge Triangles (fabric 7)	10	16	18	18	20	12	10
Corner Triangles (fabric 7)	4	4	4	4	4	4	4
Cut widths							
1st border	5″	2″	2″	2″	2″	$1^{1}/_{2}$″	2″
2nd border	—	$3^{1}/_{2}$″	$3^{1}/_{2}$″	$3^{1}/_{2}$″	$3^{1}/_{2}$″	5″	3″
3rd border	—	$6^{1}/_{2}$″	$6^{1}/_{2}$″	$7^{1}/_{2}$″	2″	—	6″
4th border	—	—	—	—	8″	—	—

General Information

	CR	TW	D	Q	K	SQ	OB
Blocks Across	3	4	5	5	6	4	3
Blocks Down	4	6	6	6	6	4	4
Total	18	39	50	50	61	25	18

Fan
Instructions

Cutting Note: All *fabric used for A must be stacked* right side up.

Piecing

A. Piecing blocks:

Step 1. Press outer edge of cone ¼″ to wrong side (Fig. 1).

Step 2. Join cones, stitching across pressed end of cones (Fig. 2).

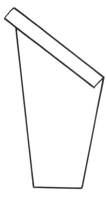 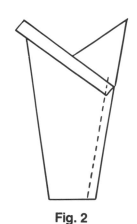

Fig. 1   **Fig. 2**

Step 3. Press seams toward long side, pressing under unstitched edge also. Trim corner (Fig. 3).

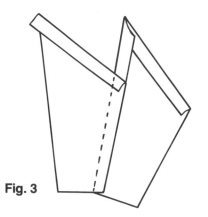

Fig. 3

Step 4. Pin fan to block.

Step 5. With running stitch and pressing template, prepare piece B for appliqué (Fig. 4). Pin on corner of fan (Fig. 5).

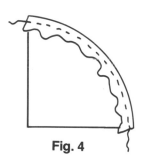 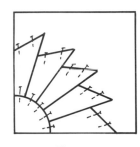

Fig. 4   **Fig. 5**

Step 6. Machine or hand appliqué pinned edges.

B. Joining blocks and triangles:

Step 1. Join units to form strips (Fig. 6).

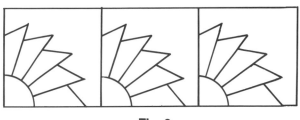

Fig. 6

Step 2. Join strips.

C. Add borders.

Finishing

A. Quilt as desired.

B. Turn 1½″ of outer border to back of quilt. Turn under ½″. Pin and stitch.

Yardages

Fabrics	CR	TW	D	Q	K	SQ	OB
1 (B)	1/4	1/2	3/4	3/4	3/4	1/2	1/4
2 thru 6, each (A)	3/8	5/8	7/8	7/8	1	1/2	3/8
7 (background squares)	2	4 1/4	5 1/4	5 1/4	6 1/2	3	2
7 (edge and corner triangles)	3/4	1 1/4	1 1/4	1 1/2	1 3/4	1	3/4
1st border	1 1/4	3/4	3/4	3/4	3/4	1/2	1/2
2nd border	—	1	1 1/4	1 1/4	1 1/2	1 1/4	3/4
3rd border	—	1 3/4	2	2 1/4	3/4	—	1 1/2
4th border	—	—	—	—	3	—	—
Backing	3 1/4	6 3/4	8 1/2	8 1/2	10 1/4	4	3 3/4

Cutting Borders

• To cut length of outer borders, add 6″ to finished sizes of quilt.
• Cut all other borders to finished quilt size.
• Trim as needed.
• All outer borders include 1 1/2″ extra to turn back for finished edge.

Yardage Notes

• All yardages include a small amount for shrinkage and waste.
• Yardages are for pieced borders, to conserve fabric. You may prefer an unpieced border, especially on wider borders. Use the longest side of your finished quilt to determine how many yards to buy.

Options

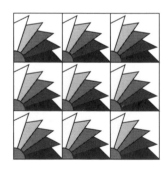

Fan
Design Page

For quick reference or design-your-own:

1. Copy this page.
2. Trim copy to desired quilt size.
3. Color design.

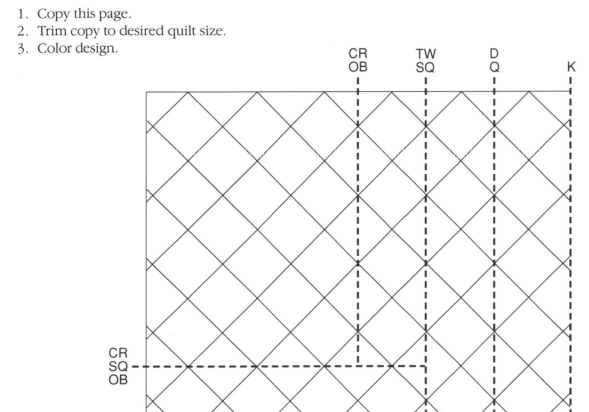

7. TUMBLING BLOCKS
Beginner

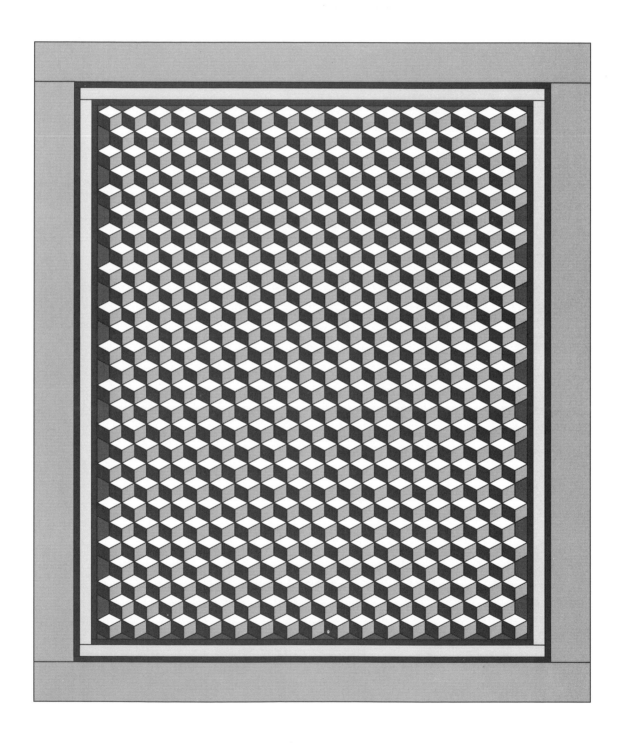

Dimensions (Inches)

	CR	TW	D	Q	K	SQ	OB
Finished Quilt	42 × 56	72 × 102	83 × 106	91 × 106	107 × 108	66 × 68	58 × 76
Center	32 × 46	52 × 82	59 × 82	67 × 82	81 × 82	56 × 58	46 × 64
1st border	1½	1½	1½	1½	1½	1½	1½
2nd border	3½	3	3	3	4	3½	4½
3rd border	—	5½	1½	1½	1½	—	—
4th border	—	—	6	6	6	—	—

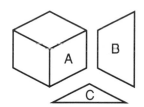

To Speed-Cut:
  A. Diamond, 60°
  B. Anvil, 60°
  C. Triangle, 60°

Cutting Instructions

	CR	TW	D	Q	K	SQ	OB
Number needed							
A (fabrics 1 thru 3, each)	128	392	446	500	608	295	263
B (fabric 4)	14	26	26	26	26	18	20
C (fabric 4)	20	32	36	40	48	34	28
Cut widths							
1st border	2″	2″	2″	2″	2″	2″	2″
2nd border	5½″	3½″	3½″	3½″	4½″	5½″	6½″
3rd border	—	7½″	2″	2″	2″	—	—
4th border	—	—	8″	8″	8″	—	—

General Information

	CR	TW	D	Q	K	SQ	OB
Units Across	9	15	17	19	23	16	13
Units Down (rows)	15	27	27	27	27	19	21
Total	128	392	446	500	608	295	263

Tumbling Blocks Instructions

Piecing

Note: *Two optional piecing methods are presented here. Method 1 is less complicated to follow, but all seams are set-in seams. Method 2 requires more planning but is faster to sew.*

A. Piecing and joining units:

Method 1

Step 1. Piece block units (Fig. 1).

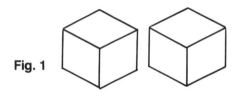

Fig. 1

Step 2. Connect blocks to form rows (Fig. 2).

Fig. 2

Step 3. Join rows (Fig. 3).

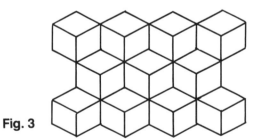

Fig. 3

Method 2

Step 1. Piece star units (Fig. 4).

Step 2. Add diamonds on three sides (Fig. 5).

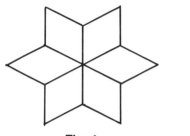

Fig. 4   **Fig. 5**

Step 3. Join units to form columns (Fig. 6).

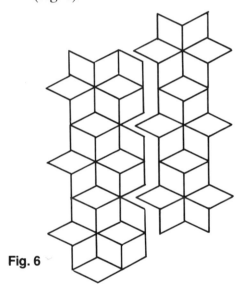

Fig. 6

Step 4. Join columns, adding additional diamonds, as needed.

B. Adding side edges, both methods:

Step 1. Insert B pieces along both sides (Fig. 7).

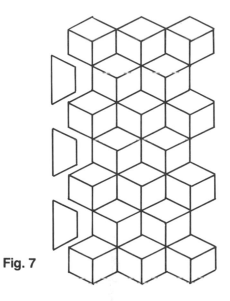

Fig. 7

Step 2. Insert C pieces along top and bottom edges (Fig. 8).

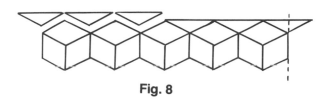

Fig. 8

Finishing

A. Quilt as desired.
B. Turn 1½″ of outer border to back of quilt. Turn under ½″. Pin and stitch.

Yardages

Fabrics	CR	TW	D	Q	K	SQ	OB
1 (A, dark)	⅞	2⅛	2¼	2⅝	3⅛	1¾	1½
2 (A, medium)	⅞	2⅛	2¼	2⅝	3⅛	1¾	1½
3 (A, light)	⅞	2⅛	2¼	2⅝	3⅛	1¾	1½
4 (B and C)	⅜	½	½	⅝	⅝	⅜	⅜
1st border	½	½	¾	¾	¾	¾	½
2nd border	1¼	1	1¼	1¼	1¾	1½	1½
3rd border	—	2	¾	¾	¾	—	—
4th border	—	—	2½	2½	3	—	—
Backing	3¼	6¾	8½	8½	10¼	4	3¾

Cutting Borders

- To cut length of outer borders, add 6″ to finished sizes of quilt.
- Cut all other borders to finished quilt size.
- Trim as needed.
- All outer borders include 1½″ extra to turn back for finished edge.

Yardage Notes

- All yardages include a small amount for shrinkage and waste.
- Yardages are for pieced borders, to conserve fabric. You may prefer an unpieced border, especially on wider borders. Use the longest side of your finished quilt to determine how many yards to buy.

Options

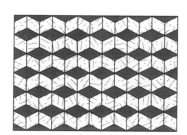

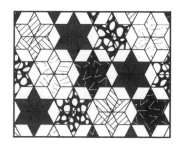

Tumbling Blocks
Design Page

For quick reference or design-your-own:

1. Copy this page.
2. Trim copy to desired quilt size.
3. Color design.

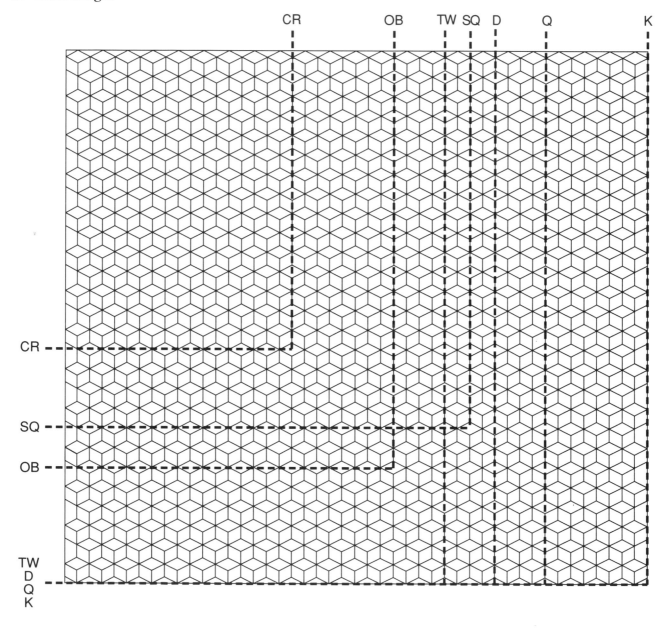

8. INDIAN STAR
Intermediate

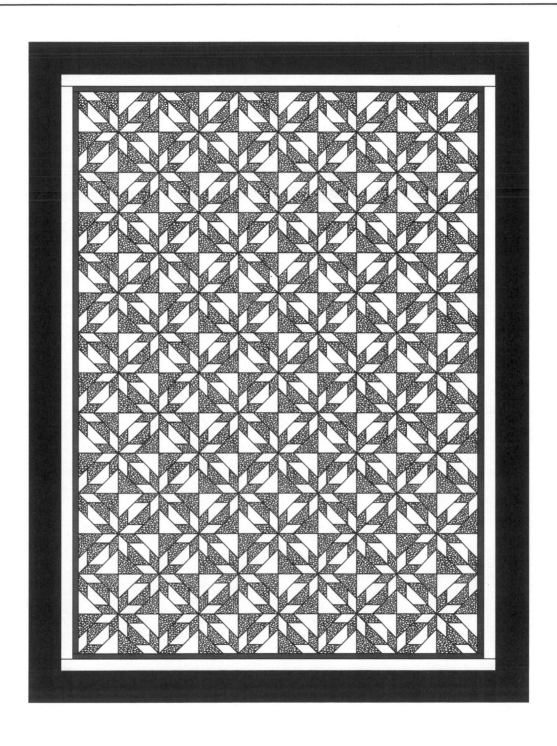

Dimensions (Inches)

	CR	TW	D	Q	K	SQ	OB
Finished Quilt	48 × 60	70 × 106	84 × 108	86 × 110	108 × 108	64 × 64	60 × 72
Center	36 × 48	48 × 84	60 × 84	60 × 84	84 × 84	48 × 48	48 × 60
1st border	1½	1½	1½	1½	1½	1½	1½
2nd border	4½	2½	2½	3	2½	6½	4½
3rd border	—	7	8	8½	8	—	—

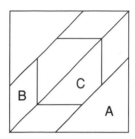

To Speed-Cut:
   A. Triangle, 45°
   B. Anvil, 45°
   C. Diamond, 45°

Cutting Instructions

	CR	TW	D	Q	K	SQ	OB
Number needed							
A (fabrics 1 and 2, each)	48	112	140	140	196	64	80
B (fabrics 1 and 2, each)	96	224	280	280	392	128	160
C (fabrics 1 and 2, each)	48	112	140	140	196	64	80
Cut widths							
Cut 1st border	2″	2″	2″	2″	2″	2″	2″
Cut 2nd border	6½″	3″	3″	3½″	3″	8½″	6½″
Cut 3rd border	—	9″	10″	10½″	10″	—	—

General Information

	CR	TW	D	Q	K	SQ	OB
Blocks Across	6	8	10	10	14	8	8
Blocks Down	8	14	14	14	14	8	10
Total	48	112	140	140	196	64	80

Indian Star
Instructions

Cutting note: *If speed-cutting, all strips used for B and C must be cut on the lengthwise grain.*

Piecing

A. Piecing Basic Units:

Step 1. Join B and C pieces, using *bias* edge of C for the seam (Fig. 1).

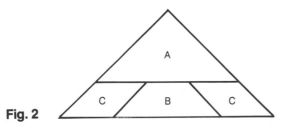

Fig. 1

Step 2. Add A pieces (Fig. 2).

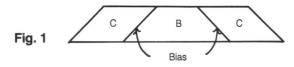

Fig. 2

Step 3. Join triangles to form basic unit (Fig. 3).

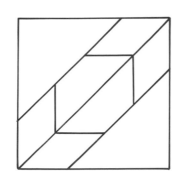

Fig. 3

B. Joining Units:

Step 1. Join 4 units to form squares (Fig. 4).

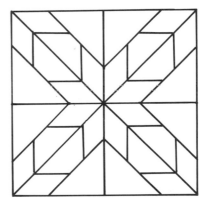

Fig. 4

Step 2. Sew squares together.

C. Add borders.

Finishing

A. Quilt as desired.
B. Turn 1½" of outer border to back of quilt. Turn under ½". Pin and stitch.

Yardages

Fabrics	CR	TW	D	Q	K	SQ	OB
1 (dark)	2	$3^5/_8$	$4^1/_2$	$4^1/_2$	$6^1/_8$	$2^1/_4$	$2^3/_4$
2 (light)	2	$3^5/_8$	$4^1/_2$	$4^1/_2$	$6^1/_8$	$2^1/_4$	$2^3/_4$
1st border	$^1/_2$	$^1/_2$	$^3/_4$	$^3/_4$	$^7/_8$	$^1/_2$	$^1/_2$
2nd border	$1^1/_2$	1	$1^1/_8$	$1^1/_3$	$1^1/_4$	$1^3/_4$	$1^1/_2$
3rd border	—	$2^1/_2$	3	$3^1/_4$	$3^1/_2$	—	—
Backing	3	$6^1/_4$	8	$8^1/_4$	$9^3/_4$	4	$3^3/_4$

Cutting Borders

- To cut length of outer borders, add 6″ to finished sizes of quilt.
- Cut all other borders to finished quilt size.
- Trim as needed.
- All outer borders include 1½″ extra to turn back for finished edge.

Yardage Notes

- All yardages include a small amount for shrinkage and waste.
- Yardages are for pieced borders, to conserve fabric. You may prefer an unpieced border, especially on wider borders. Use the longest side of your finished quilt to determine how many yards to buy.

Options

Indian Star
Design Page

For quick reference or design-your-own:

1. Copy this page.
2. Trim copy to desired quilt size.
3. Color design.

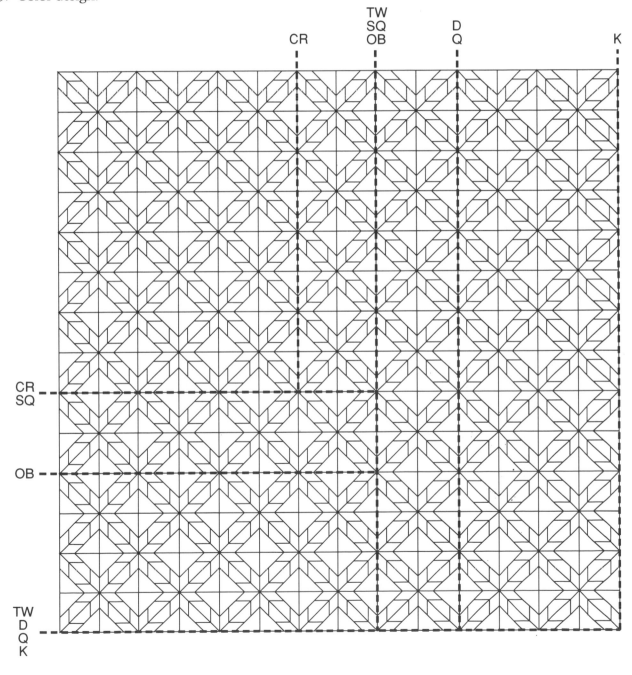

9. ALL TIED UP
Intermediate

Dimensions (Inches)

	CR	TW	D	Q	K	SQ	OB
Finished Quilt	48 × 60	70 × 106	84 × 108	86 × 110	108 × 108	64 × 64	60 × 72
Center	42 × 54	59 × 95	72 × 96	73 × 97	96 × 96	56 × 56	54 × 66
1st border	2	1½	1½	1½	1½	1½	2
2nd border	4	3	3	4	3	2½	4
3rd border	—	1½	1½	1½	1½	4	—
4th border	—	5	6	6	6	—	—

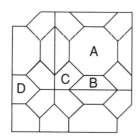

To Speed-Cut:
   A. Octagon
   B. Anvil, 45°
   C, D. Candle, 45°

Cutting Instructions

	CR	TW	D	Q	K	SQ	OB
Number needed							
A (fabric 3)	48	112	140	140	196	64	80
B (fabric 2)	164	404	512	512	728	221	284
C (fabric 1)	188	444	556	556	780	252	316
D (fabric 3)	28	44	48	48	56	36	36
Cut widths							
Cut 1st border	2½"	2"	2"	2"	2"	2"	2½"
Cut 2nd border	6"	3½"	3½"	4½"	3½"	3"	6"
Cut 3rd border	—	2"	2"	2"	2"	6"	—
Cut 4th border	—	7"	8"	8"	8"	—	—

General Information

	CR	TW	D	Q	K	SQ	OB
Blocks Across	5	7	9	9	13	7	7
Blocks Down	7	13	13	13	13	7	9
Total	35	91	117	117	169	49	63

All Tied Up
Instructions

Piecing

A. Piecing basic units:

Step 1. Center C pieces on short sides of A piece (Fig. 1).

Step 2. With A on top, stitch as shown (Fig. 2).

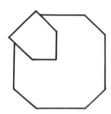

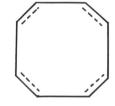

Fig. 1   **Fig. 2**

Step 3. With A on top, inset B pieces on remaining sides (Fig. 3).

Step 4. Join B and C pieces (Fig. 4).

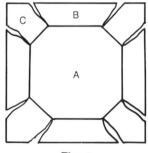

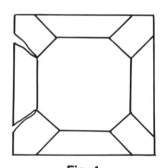

Fig. 3   **Fig. 4**

Step 5. Join squares (Fig. 5).

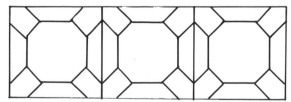

Fig. 5

B. Piecing outer rows:

Note: *One outer row of "half-units" is added to complete the design and create a lovely, floating look.*

Step 1. Cut A pieces in half, as needed, for edge pieces (Fig. 6). Cut one A piece in fourths for corners (Fig. 7).

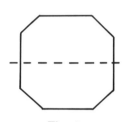

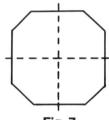

Fig. 6   **Fig. 7**

Step 2. Join pieces as shown (Fig. 8).

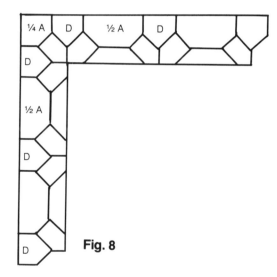

Fig. 8

Step 3. Add outer rows to quilt (Fig. 9).

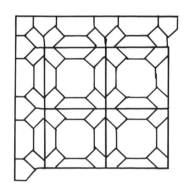

Fig. 9

C. Add borders.

Finishing

A. Quilt as desired.
B. Turn 1½" of outer border to back of quilt. Turn under ½". Pin and stitch.

Yardages

Fabrics	CR	TW	D	Q	K	SQ	OB
1 (C)	1	2	2³/₈	2³/₈	3¼	1¼	1⅛
2 (B)	1	2	2½	2½	1¼	½	⅝
3 (A, D)	1¼	2¼	2⅝	2⅝	3½	1¼	1¾
1st border	¾	¾	¾	¾	¾	¾	¾
2nd border	1½	1	1¼	1½	1½	1	1½
3rd border	—	¾	¾	¾	¾	1½	—
4th border	—	2	2½	2½	3	—	—
Backing	3¼	6¾	8½	8½	10¼	4	3¾

Cutting Borders

• To cut length of outer borders, add 6″ to finished sizes of quilt.
• Cut all other borders to finished quilt size.
• Trim as needed.
• All outer borders include 1½″ extra to turn back for finished edge.

Yardage Notes

• All yardages include a small amount for shrinkage and waste.
• Yardages are for pieced borders, to conserve fabric. You may prefer an unpieced border, especially on wider borders. Use the longest side of your finished quilt to determine how many yards to buy.

Options

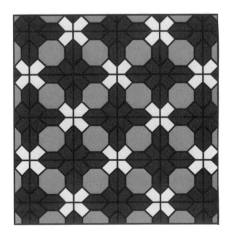

All Tied Up
Design Page

For quick reference or design-your-own:

1. Copy this page.
2. Trim copy to desired quilt size.
3. Color design.

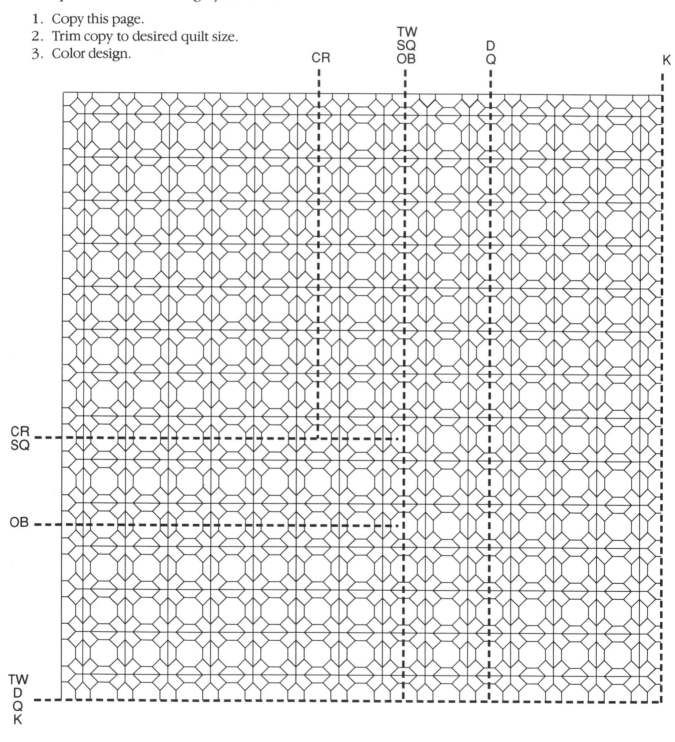

10. DRUNKARD'S PATH
Intermediate

Dimensions (Inches)

	CR	TW	D	Q	K	SQ	OB
Finished Quilt	48 × 60	70 × 102	68 × 102	90 × 106	106 × 106	64 × 64	60 × 72
Center	36 × 48	48 × 80	64 × 80	64 × 80	80 × 80	48 × 48	48 × 60
1st border	2	1½	1½	1½	1½	1½	2
2nd border	4	3	3	4	4	2½	4
3rd border	—	1½	1½	1½	1½	4	—
4th border	—	5	5	6	6	—	—

To Speed-Cut:
A. Bite
B. Fan

Cutting Instructions

	CR	TW	D	Q	K	SQ	OB
Size of square	3″	4″	4″	4″	5″	3″	3″
Number needed							
A (fabrics 1 and 2, each)	96	120	160	160	128	128	160
B (fabrics 1 and 2, each)	96	120	160	160	128	128	160
Cut widths							
Cut 1st border	2½″	2″	2″	2″	2″	2″	2½″
Cut 2nd border	6″	3½″	3½″	4½″	4½″	3″	6″
Cut 3rd border	—	2″	2″	2″	2″	6″	—
Cut 4th border	—	7″	7″	8″	8″	—	—

General Information

	CR	TW	D	Q	K	SQ	OB
Blocks Across	12	12	16	16	16	16	16
Blocks Down	16	20	20	20	16	16	20
Total	192	240	320	320	256	256	320

Drunkard's Path Instructions

Piecing

A. Piecing basic units:

Step 1. Center piece B on piece A. Pin at center (Fig. 1).

Step 2. With A on top and stretching fabric as needed, stitch from one edge to the pin (Fig. 2). With needle in fabric, match corners. Finish stitching seam (Fig. 3). You may want to pin the ends if you have trouble keeping them lined up.

Note: *There is no need to clip these curved seams as the "puckery" look will be absorbed in the quilting.*

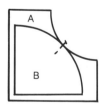

Fig. 1   **Fig. 2**   **Fig. 3**

B. Joining the units:

  Step 1. Join 4 units to form squares (Fig. 4).

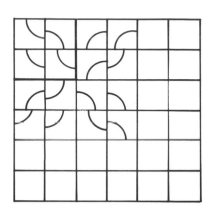

Fig. 5

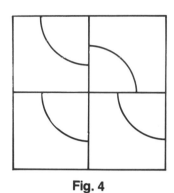

Fig. 4

  Step 2. Join squares (Fig. 5).

C. Add borders.

Finishing

A. Quilt as desired.
B. Turn 1½″ of outer border to back of quilt. Turn under ½″. Pin and stitch.

Yardages

Fabrics	CR	TW	D	Q	K	SQ	OB
1 (dark)	1½	3⅛	3¾	3¾	4¾	2	2½
2 (light)	1½	3⅛	3¾	3¾	4¾	2	2½
1st border	¾	¾	¾	¾	¾	¾	¾
2nd border	1½	1	1¼	1½	2	1	1½
3rd border	—	¾	¾	¾	¾	1½	—
4th border	—	2	2¼	2½	3	—	—
Backing	3¼	6¾	8½	8½	10¼	4	3¾

Cutting Borders

• To cut length of outer borders, add 6″ to finished sizes of quilt.
• Cut all other borders to finished quilt size.
• Trim as needed.
• All outer borders include 1½″ extra to turn back for finished edge.

Yardage Notes

• All yardages include a small amount for shrinkage and waste.
• Yardages are for pieced borders, to conserve fabric. You may prefer an unpieced border, especially on wider borders. Use the longest side of your finished quilt to determine how many yards to buy.

Options

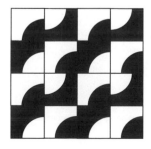

Drunkard's Path
Design Page

For quick reference or design-your-own:

1. Copy this page.
2. Trim copy to desired quilt size.
3. Color design.

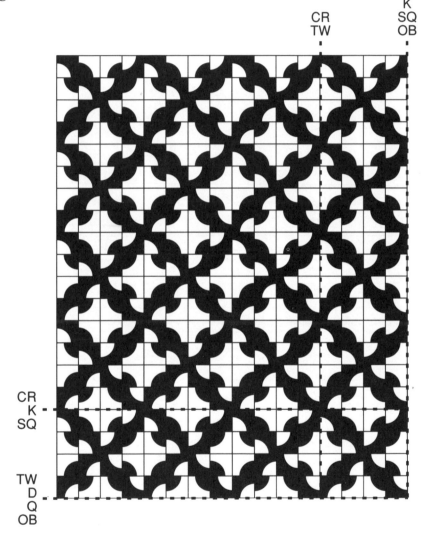

11. NIGHTTIME
Intermediate

Dimensions (Inches)

	CR	TW	D	Q	K	SQ	OB
Finished Quilt	42 × 52	69 × 106	86 × 106	92 × 105	111 × 106	65 × 58	61 × 69
Center	34 × 44	51 × 88	68 × 88	68 × 81	93 × 88	51 × 44	51 × 59
1st border	4	1¹⁄₂	1¹⁄₂	1¹⁄₂	1¹⁄₂	1¹⁄₂	1¹⁄₂
2nd border	—	2¹⁄₂	2¹⁄₂	2¹⁄₂	2¹⁄₂	5¹⁄₂	3¹⁄₂
3rd border	—	5	5	8	5	—	—

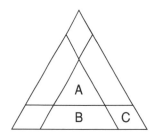

To Speed-Cut:
  A. Triangle, 60°
  B. Anvil, 60°
  C. Diamond, 60°

Cutting Instructions

	CR	TW	D	Q	K	SQ	OB
Number needed							
C (fabric 1, light)	162	468	612	564	828	234	312
B (fabric 2, light med.)	81	234	306	282	414	117	156
B (fabric 3, dark med.)	81	234	306	282	414	117	156
A (fabric 4, dark)	54	156	204	187	276	78	104
Cut widths							
Cut 1st border	6″	2″	2″	2″	2″	2″	2″
Cut 2nd border	—	3″	3″	3″	3″	7¹⁄₂″	5¹⁄₂″
Cut 3rd border	—	7″	7″	10″	7″	—	—

General Information

	CR	TW	D	Q	K	SQ	OB
Units across	9	13	17	17	23	13	13
Units down (rows)	6	12	12	11	12	6	8
Total	54	156	204	187	276	78	104

Nighttime Instructions

Cutting Notes: In speed-cutting, all strips used for B and C must be cut on the lengthwise grain.

Piecing

A. Piecing basic units:

Step 1. Join pieces in sets (Fig. 1).

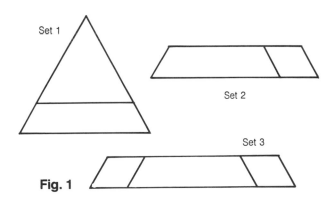

Fig. 1

Step 2. Join sets 1 and 2 (Fig. 2).

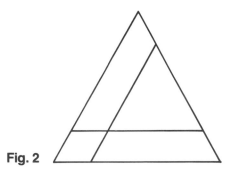

Fig. 2

Step 3. Add set 3 (Fig. 3).

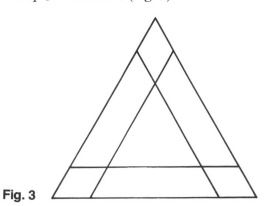

Fig. 3

B. Joining the units:

Step 1. Combine units to form rows (Fig. 4).

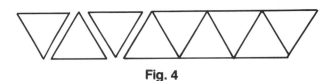

Fig. 4

Step 2. Join rows (Fig. 5).

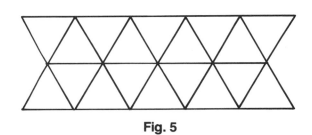

Fig. 5

Step 3. Trim side edges (Fig. 6).

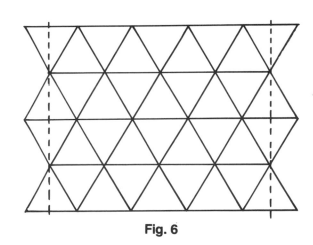

Fig. 6

C. Add borders.

Finishing

A. Quilt as desired.
B. Turn 1½″ of outer border to back of quilt. Turn under ½″. Pin and stitch.

Yardages

Fabrics	CR	TW	D	Q	K	SQ	OB
1 (C, light)	3/4	1 1/2	2 1/4	2 1/4	3	1	1 1/4
2 (B, light med.)	7/8	2	2 1/2	2 1/2	3 1/4	1 1/8	1 1/2
3 (B, dark med.)	7/8	2	2 1/2	2 1/2	3 1/4	1 1/8	1 1/2
4 (A, dark)	5/8	1 5/8	2	2	2 1/2	1	1 1/8
1st border	3/4	3/4	3/4	3/4	3/4	3/4	1/2
2nd border	—	1	1	1 1/4	1 1/2	1 1/2	1 1/4
3rd border	—	—	2	3	2 3/4	—	—
Backing	2 1/2	6 1/4	8	8	10	3 1/2	3 3/4

Cutting Borders

- To cut length of outer borders, add 6″ to finished sizes of quilt.
- Cut all other borders to finished quilt size.
- Trim as needed.
- All outer borders include 1 1/2″ extra to turn back for finished edge.

Yardage Notes

- All yardages include a small amount for shrinkage and waste.
- Yardages are for pieced borders, to conserve fabric. You may prefer an unpieced border, especially on wider borders. Use the longest side of your finished quilt to determine how many yards to buy.

Options

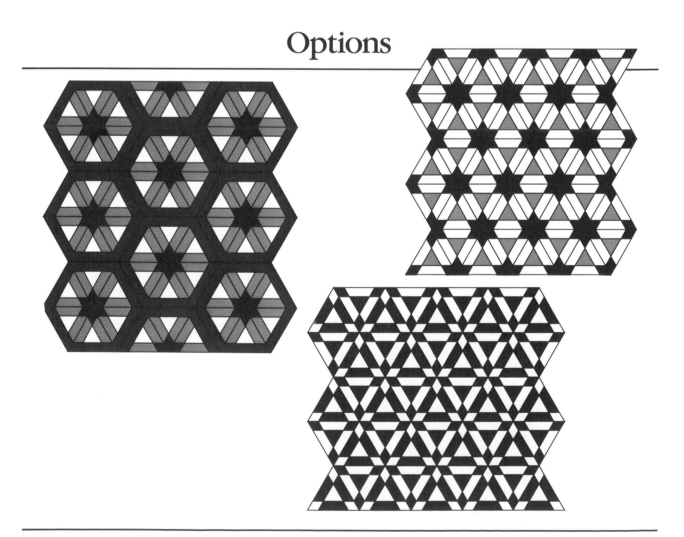

Nighttime
Design Page

For quick reference or design-your-own:

1. Copy this page.
2. Trim copy to desired quilt size.
3. Color design.

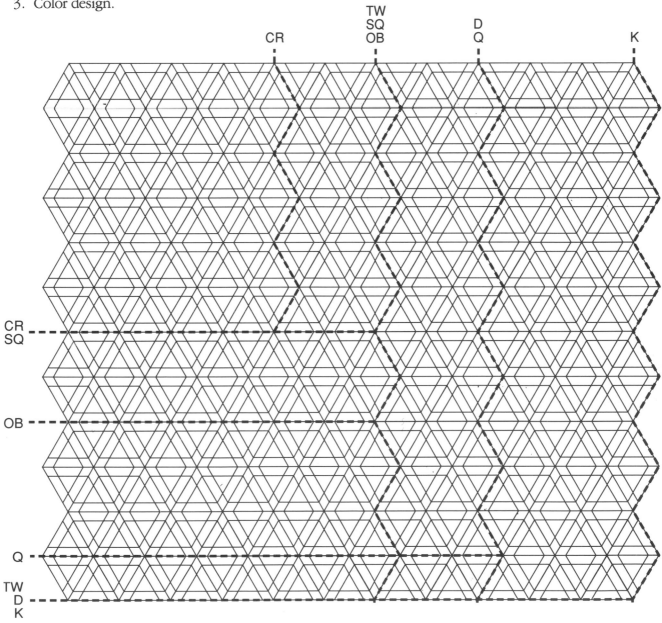

12. ALWAYS FRIENDS
Intermediate

Dimensions (Inches)

	CR	TW	D	Q	K	SQ	OB
Finished Quilt	36 × 52	73 × 102	86 × 102	92 × 108	105 × 108	67 × 71	61 × 77

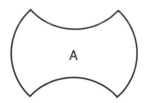

To Speed-Cut:
A. Ax-head

Cutting Instructions

	CR	TW	D	Q	K	SQ	OB
Number needed							
A (fabrics 1 and 2, each)	94	380	446	508	578	242	238
Cut binding (bias)				2½″ wide			

General Information

	CR	TW	D	Q	K	SQ	OB
Blocks Across	11	23	27	29	33	21	19
Blocks Down	17	33	33	35	35	23	25
Total	187	759	891	1015	1155	483	475

Always Friends Instructions

Piecing

A. Piecing units:

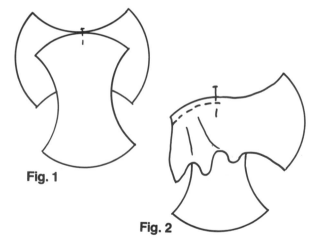

Fig. 1

Fig. 2

Step 1. Center curved sections as shown (Fig. 1). Pin at center point.

Step 2. Turn unit over so inner curve is now on top (Fig. 2). Stitch.

Note: *If you are new at sewing curved seams, refer to the section about sewing curves in Chapter 5. Stitch a few practice pieces first!*

Step 3. Join pieces in rows (Fig. 3).

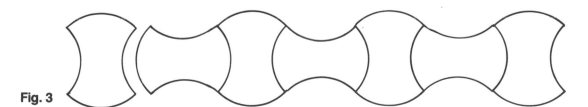

Fig. 3

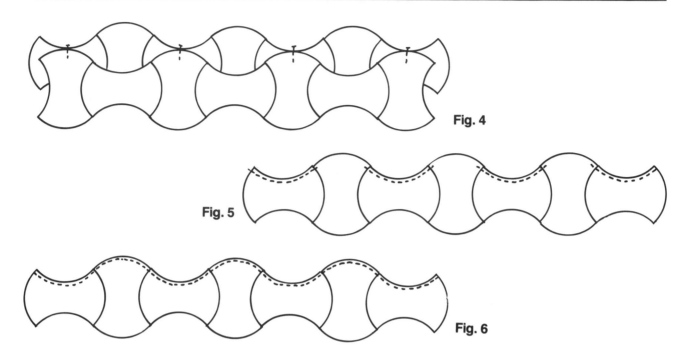

Fig. 4

Fig. 5

Fig. 6

Note: *There is no need to clip these curved seams as the "puckery" look will be absorbed in the quilting.*

B. Joining the rows:

Step 1. Place two rows together, pinning centers of every other curve (Fig. 4).

Step 2. Stitch *pinned curves only,* starting and ending about ¹/₄″ past each seam (Fig. 5). (I find it easier and faster to pin the seams, too).

Step 3. Turn piece over. Stitch remaining portions of seam (Fig. 6).

Finishing

A. Quilt as desired.
B. Cut bias binding 2¹/₂″ wide. Bind, following curved edges.

Yardages

Fabrics	CR	TW	D	Q	K	SQ	OB
1 (A, dark)	1³/₄	5³/₄	6³/₄	7⁵/₈	8⁵/₈	3⁷/₈	3⁷/₈
2 (A, light)	1³/₄	5³/₄	6³/₄	7⁵/₈	8⁵/₈	3⁷/₈	3⁷/₈
Binding	³/₄	1¹/₈	1¹/₄	1¹/₄	1¹/₂	1	1
Backing	1⁵/₈	6¹/₄	7³/₄	8¹/₄	10	4¹/₄	3³/₄

Yardage Notes

• All yardages include a small amount for shrinkage and waste.

Options

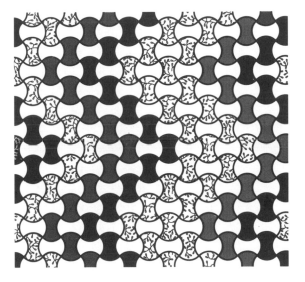

Always Friends
Design Page

For quick reference or design-your-own:

1. Copy this page.
2. Trim copy to desired quilt size.
3. Color design.

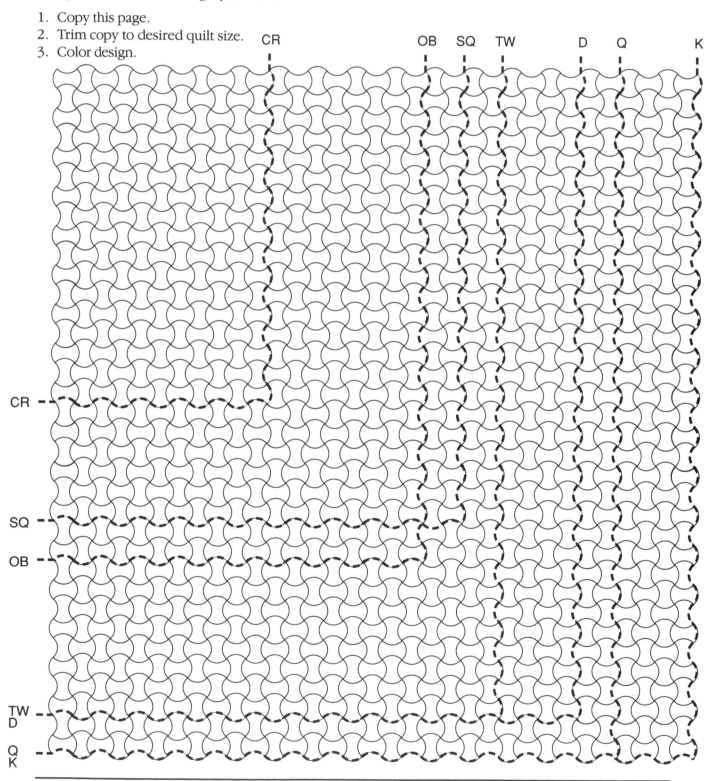

13. PEACOCK
Intermediate

Dimensions (Inches)

	CR	TW	D	Q	K	SQ	OB
Finished Quilt	48 × 60	70 × 106	84 × 108	86 × 110	108 × 108	64 × 64	60 × 72
Center	36 × 48	48 × 84	60 × 84	60 × 84	84 × 84	48 × 48	48 × 60
1st border	2	1½	1½	1½	1½	1½	2
2nd border	4	3	3	4	3	2½	4
3rd border	—	1½	1½	1½	1½	4	—
4th border	—	5	6	6	6	—	—

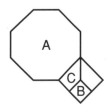

To Speed-Cut:
  A. Octagon
  B. Square
  C. Shoe, 45°

Cutting Instructions

	CR	TW	D	Q	K	SQ	OB
Number needed							
A (fabric 3)*	48	112	140	140	196	64	80
B (fabric 1)	48	112	140	140	196	64	80
C (fabric 2)†	96	224	280	280	392	128	160
Cut widths							
Cut 1st border	2½"	2"	2"	2"	2"	2"	2½"
Cut 2nd border	6"	3½"	3½"	4½"	3½"	3"	6"
Cut 3rd border	—	2"	2"	2"	2"	6"	—
Cut 4th border	—	7"	8"	8"	8"	—	—

General Information

	CR	TW	D	Q	K	SQ	OB
Squares Across	5	7	9	9	13	7	7
Squares Down	7	13	13	13	13	7	9
Total	35	91	117	117	169	49	63

*Number needed for piece A includes enough to cut in half for
  side "extras."
†Reverse half of C pieces.

Peacock
Instructions

Cutting Notes: *The C pieces are mirror images. Stack fabric with* like sides together.

When speed-cutting, cut strips used for A as indicated by arrow on full-sized templates (Appendix C). This uses a bit more fabric, but places the straight grain along lengths and widths of the quilt.

Piecing

A. Piecing basic units and joining rows:

Step 1. Piece units as shown (Figs. 1–3).

Fig. 1

Fig. 2

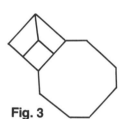
Fig. 3

Step 2. Join units to form rows (Fig. 4). Add one small unit at right end of each row.

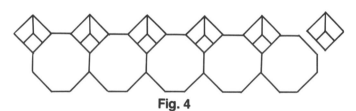
Fig. 4

Step 3. Join rows. Insert small units only for bottom row (Fig. 5).

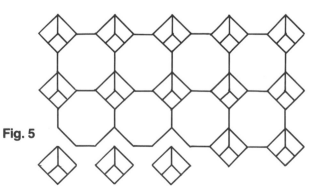
Fig. 5

B. Adding edge pieces:

Step 1. Cut A pieces in half as needed (Fig. 6). Cut one A piece in fourths for corners (Fig. 7).

Fig. 6

Fig. 7

Step 2. Insert these pieces on sides, bottom and top (Fig. 8).

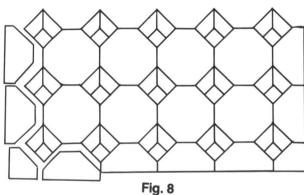
Fig. 8

C. Add borders.

Finishing

A. Quilt as desired.
B. Turn 1½″ of outer border to back of quilt. Turn under ½″. Pin and stitch.

Yardages

Fabrics	CR	TW	D	Q	K	SQ	OB
1 (B)	1/4	1/2	5/8	5/8	3/4	3/8	3/8
2 (C)	5/8	1 1/4	1 1/2	1 1/2	2	7/8	1
3 (A)	1 3/4	4	4 5/8	4 5/8	6 1/2	2 1/4	3
1st border	3/4	3/4	3/4	3/4	3/4	3/4	3/4
2nd border	1 1/2	1	1 1/4	1 1/2	1 1/2	1	1 1/2
3rd border	—	3/4	3/4	3/4	3/4	1 1/2	—
4th border	—	2	2 1/2	2 1/2	3	—	—
Backing	3 1/4	6 3/4	8 1/2	8 1/2	10 1/4	4	3 3/4

Cutting Borders

- To cut length of outer borders, add 6″ to finished sizes of quilt.
- Cut all other borders to finished quilt size.
- Trim as needed.
- All outer borders include 1 1/2″ extra to turn back for finished edge.

Yardage Notes

- All yardages include a small amount for shrinkage and waste.
- Yardages are for pieced borders, to conserve fabric. You may prefer an unpieced border, especially on wider borders. Use the longest side of your finished quilt to determine how many yards to buy.

Options

  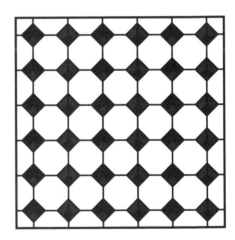

Peacock
Design Page

For quick reference or design-your-own:

1. Copy this page.
2. Trim copy to desired quilt size.
3. Color design.

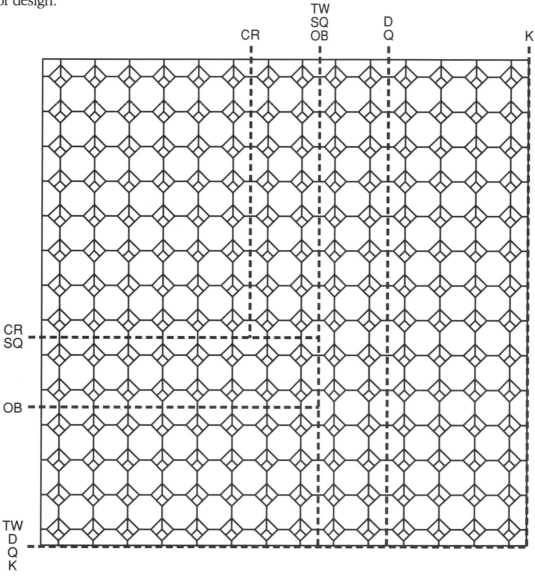

14. MAGNOLIAS
Intermediate

Dimensions (Inches)

	CR	TW	D	Q	K	SQ	OB
Finished Quilt	43 × 55	70 × 104	84 × 106	88 × 110	108 × 108	65 × 65	57 × 80
Center	33 × 45	56 × 90	68 × 90	68 × 90	90 × 90	45 × 45	45 × 68
1st border	1½	2	1½	1½	1½	1½	2
2nd border	3½	5	2½	3	3	3	4
3rd border	—	—	4	5½	4½	5½	—

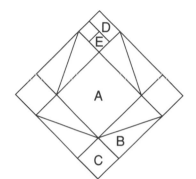

Cut squares for:
Edge triangles: 9″ × 9″
Corner triangles: 6½″ × 6½″

To Speed-Cut:
A,C,E. Square
D. Rectangle
B. Triangle, 45°
B. Clipped points

Cutting Instructions

	CR	TW	D	Q	K	SQ	OB
Number needed							
A (fabric 2)	18	68	83	83	113	25	39
B (fabrics 2 and 3, each)*	36	136	166	166	226	50	78
B (fabric 4)	72	272	332	332	452	100	156
C (fabric 4)	54	204	249	249	339	75	117
D (fabric 4)	18	68	83	83	113	25	39
E (fabrics 1 and 4, each)	18	68	83	83	113	25	39
Edge triangles (fabric 4)	10	22	24	24	28	12	16
Corner triangles (fabric 4)	4	4	4	4	4	4	4
Cut widths							
Cut 1st border	2″	2½″	2″	2″	2″	2″	2½″
Cut 2nd border	5½″	7″	3″	3½″	3½″	3½″	6″
Cut 3rd border	—	—	6″	7½″	6½″	7½″	—

*Reverse half of B pieces.

General Information

	CR	TW	D	Q	K	SQ	OB
Blocks across	3	5	6	6	8	4	4
Blocks down	4	8	8	8	8	4	6
Total	18	68	83	83	113	25	39

Magnolias
Instructions

Cutting Notes: *The B pieces are mirror images. Stack fabric with like sides together.*

Piecing

A. Piecing blocks:

Step 1. Join B pieces, matching clipped points to square corners (Fig. 1).

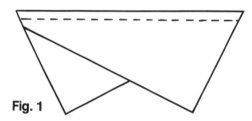

Fig. 1

Note: *When pressing, you'll see a tiny "bite" out of each corner (Fig. 2). These are rather strange-looking units, but they work—your triangles will match like magic!*

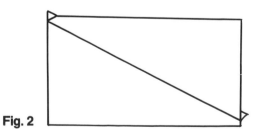

Fig. 2

Step 2. Join bud units (Fig. 3).

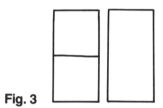

Fig. 3

Step 3. Join units (Fig. 4).

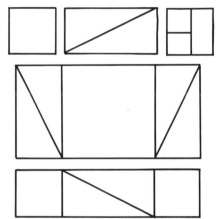

Fig. 4

Note: *When stitching triangle units to other units, begin seam at corner with "bite" out.*

B. Joining blocks and triangles:

Step 1. Join units to form strips (Fig. 5).

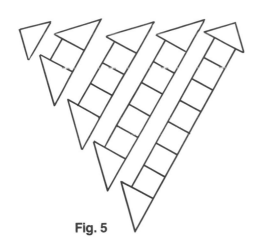

Fig. 5

Step 2. Join strips.

C. Add borders.

Finishing

A. Quilt as desired.
B. Turn 1½″ of outer border to back of quilt. Turn under ½″. Pin and stitch.

Yardages

Fabrics	CR	TW	D	Q	K	SQ	OB
1 (E—bud "center")	⅛	⅛	¼	¼	¼	⅛	⅛
2 (A and B—magnolia)	1	2¼	2¾	2¾	3½	1¼	1½
3 (B—leaves)	⅜	1	1¼	1¼	1½	½	⅝
4 (B, C, D, E—background)	1¼	3¼	4	4	5½	1¾	2
4 (triangles)	¾	1	1¼	1¼	1½	¾	1
1st border	½	¾	¾	¾	¾	¾	¾
2nd border	1¼	2	1	1¼	1½	1	1½
3rd border	—	—	2	2¼	2½	2	—
Backing	3	6½	7¾	8¾	10½	4¼	3¾

Cutting Borders

• To cut length of outer borders, add 6″ to finished sizes of quilt.
• Cut all other borders to finished quilt size.
• Trim as needed.
• All outer borders include 1½″ extra to turn back for finished edge.

Yardage Notes

• All yardages include a small amount for shrinkage and waste.
• Yardages are for pieced borders, to conserve fabric. You may prefer an unpieced border, especially on wider borders. Use the longest side of your finished quilt to determine how many yards to buy.

Options

Magnolias
Design Page

For quick reference or design-your-own:

1. Copy this page.
2. Trim copy to desired quilt size.
3. Color design.

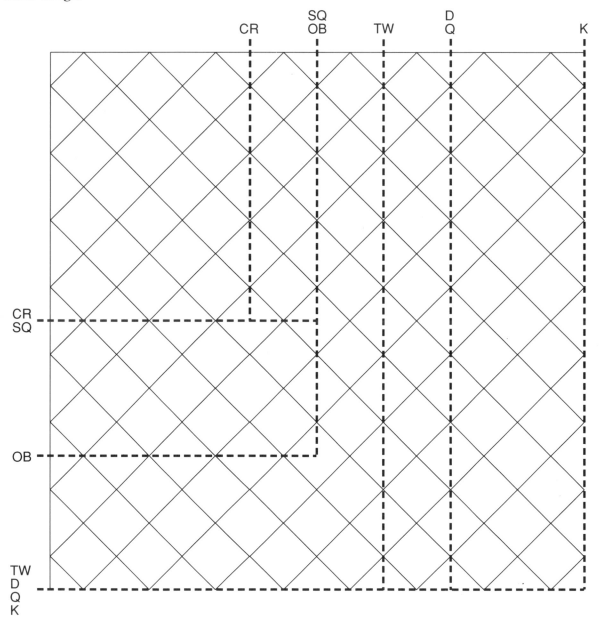

15. CLAMSHELL
Intermediate

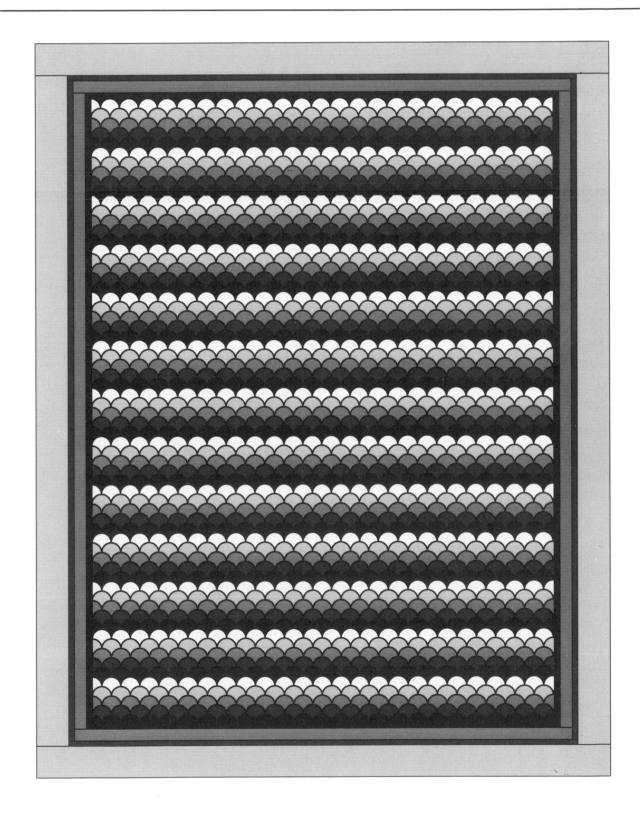

Dimensions (inches)

	CR	TW	D	Q	K	SQ	OB
Finished quilt	42 × 57	70 × 103	84 × 104	91 × 106	106 × 106	67 × 67	59 × 74
Center	30 × 45	50 × 83	60 × 80	65 × 80	80 × 80	55 × 55	43 × 58
1st border	2	1½	1½	1½	1½	2	1½
2nd border	4	3	3	4	4	4	2½
3rd border	—	5½	1½	1½	1½	—	4
4th border	—	—	6	6	6	—	—

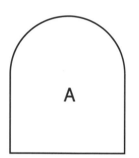

To Speed-Cut:
  A. Archway

Cutting Instructions

	CR	TW	D	Q	K	SQ	OB
Number needed							
A (fabric 1)	91	273	300	324	768	184	162
A (fabrics 2 thru 4, each)	91	273	325	338	832	207	162
A (fabric 5)	104	294	325	338	832	207	180
Starter strip (fabric 1)	4½″ × 40″	4½″ × 60″	4½″ × 70″	4½″ × 75″	4½″ × 168″	4½″ × 65″	4½″ × 53″
Cut widths							
Cut 1st border	2½″	2″	2″	2″	2″	2½″	2″
Cut 2nd border	6″	3½″	3½″	4½″	4½″	6″	3″
Cut 3rd border	—	7½″	2″	2″	2″	—	6″
Cut 4th border	—	—	8″	8″	8″	—	—

General Information

	CR	TW	D	Q	K	SQ	OB
Shells across	12	20	24	26	32	22	17
Shells down	36	66	64	64	64	44	46
Total	450	1353	1568	1696	4064	990	805

Clamshell
Instructions

Note: *The clamshell quilt is pieced from the top down. It begins with a 4½" wide strip across the entire top of the quilt. This is the starting strip and is used as a base on which to sew the first row of clamshells. The quilt is then built, row by row, down from there.*

Piecing

A. Piecing the shells:

Step 1. Join shells in rows 1" up from base (Fig. 1).

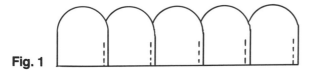

Fig. 1

Step 2. With running stitch and pressing template, prepare rounded edges for appliqué. Press seams open (Fig. 2).

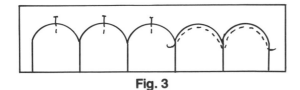

Fig. 2

Step 3. Matching base of first shell row to base of starting strip, and centering shell unit on strip, pin in place (Fig. 3). Baste curved edges.

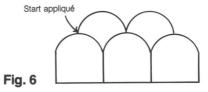

Fig. 3

Step 4. Using transparent ruler, mark 1⅝" from bottom edge of basted strip. Mark only a *tiny* point at shell joining (Fig. 4).

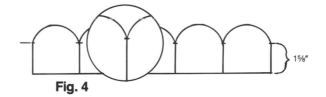

Fig. 4

1⅝"

Note: *The shells must meet neatly at this point. If they do not, adjust in final appliqué.*

Step 5. Pin and baste row 2, matching center top of each shell with mark on previous row. (Fig. 5).

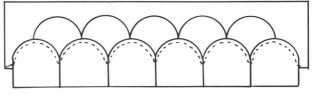

Row 1

Row 2

Fig. 5

Note: *The even-numbered rows will have an extra half-shell at each end. Appliqué only* from *center top of these shells (Fig. 6).*

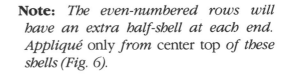

Start appliqué

Fig. 6

Step 6. Hand or machine appliqué row 1. Trim away seams on back of row. (On row 1 you'll be trimming away a bit of the starting strip, too.)

Step 7. Repeat Steps 4, 5 and 6.

Note: *When measuring 1⅝" in Step 4, check previous rows to be sure they are even and parallel with the newest row.*

B. Trimming sides: Trim away excess shells from sides, *leaving ¹/₄″ seam allowance.*

C. Add borders.

Finishing

A. Quilt as desired.

B. Turn 1¹/₂″ of outer border to back of quilt. Turn under ¹/₂″. Pin and stitch.

Yardages

Fabrics	CR	TW	D	Q	K	SQ	OB
1 (Dark)	1	2¹/₄	2¹/₂	2⁵/₈	5³/₄	1³/₄	1³/₈
2 (Medium dark)	⁷/₈	2¹/₈	2¹/₂	2⁵/₈	6	1⁵/₈	1¹/₄
3 (Medium)	⁷/₈	2¹/₈	2¹/₂	2⁵/₈	6	1⁵/₈	1¹/₄
4 (Medium light)	⁷/₈	2¹/₈	2¹/₂	2⁵/₈	6	1⁵/₈	1¹/₄
5 (Light)	1	2¹/₄	2¹/₂	2⁵/₈	6	1⁵/₈	1⁵/₈
1st border	³/₄	³/₄	³/₄	³/₄	³/₄	³/₄	¹/₂
2nd border	1¹/₂	1	1¹/₄	1¹/₂	1³/₄	1¹/₂	³/₄
3rd border	—	2	³/₄	³/₄	³/₄	—	1¹/₂
4th border	—	—	2¹/₂	2¹/₂	3	—	—
Backing	3¹/₄	6³/₄	8¹/₂	8¹/₂	10¹/₄	4	3³/₄

Cutting Borders

• To cut length of outer borders, add 6″ to finished sizes of quilt.

• Cut all other borders to finished quilt size.

• Trim as needed.

• All outer borders include 1¹/₂″ extra to turn back for finished edge.

Yardage Notes

• All yardages include a small amount for shrinkage and waste.

• Yardages are for pieced borders, to conserve fabric. You may prefer an unpieced border, especially on wider borders. Use the longest side of your finished quilt to determine how many yards to buy.

Options

Clamshell
Design Page

For quick reference or design-your-own:

1. Copy this page.
2. Trim copy to desired quilt size.
3. Color design.

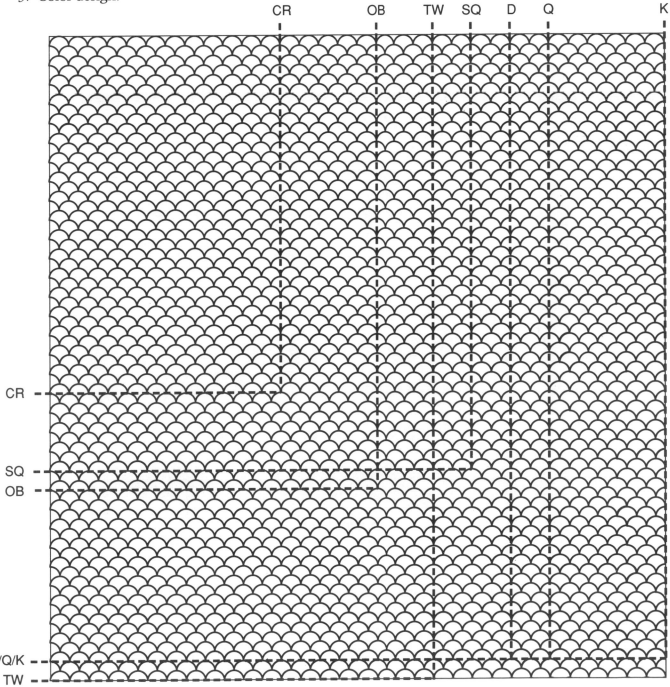

16. SIX-POINT STAR
Intermediate

Dimensions (inches)

	CR	TW	D	Q	K	SQ	OB
Finished quilt	44 × 58	69 × 104	86 × 104	90 × 108	107 × 108	65 × 62	58 × 72
Center	38 × 52	47 × 82	64 × 82	64 × 82	81 × 82	55 × 52	38 × 52
1st border	3	1½	1½	1½	1½	1½	1½
2nd border	—	3	3	3	3	3	2½
3rd border	—	6½	6½	8½	8½	—	6

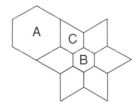

To Speed-Cut:
A, B. Hexagon
C. Gemstone, 60°

Cutting Instructions

	CR	TW	D	Q	K	SQ	OB
Number needed							
A (fabric 1)	72	132	180	180	228	104	72
B (fabric 2)	32	61	83	83	105	46	32
C (fabric 3)	198	376	508	508	640	282	198
Cut widths							
Cut 1st border	5″	2″	2″	2″	2″	2″	2″
Cut 2nd border	—	3½″	3½″	3½″	3½″	5″	3″
Cut 3rd border	—	8½″	8½″	10½″	10½″	—	8″

General Information

	CR	TW	D	Q	K	SQ	OB
Unit "Columns" Across	9	11	15	15	19	13	9
"Stars" Down	4	6	6	6	6	4	4
Total Units	32	61	83	83	105	46	32

Six-Point Star Instructions

Piecing

Note: *Hand piecing the star units will be faster and easier than machine piecing. You'll probably want to hand piece the remainder of the quilt, too. If, however, speed is important, the longer seams may be machine pieced very nicely.*

A. Piecing basic units:

Step 1. Join star units (Fig. 1).

Step 2. Add large hexagons (Fig. 2).

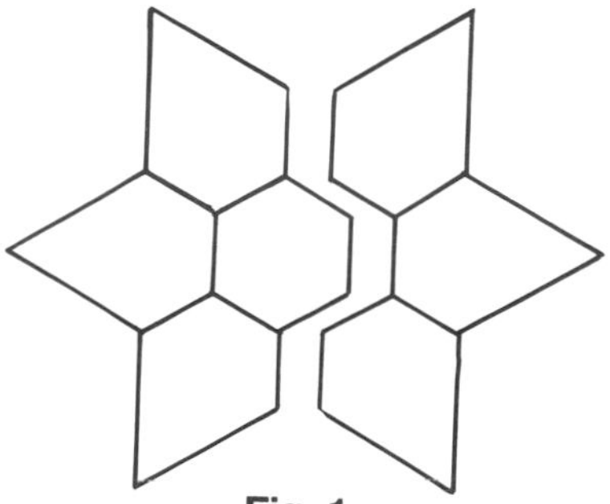

Fig. 1

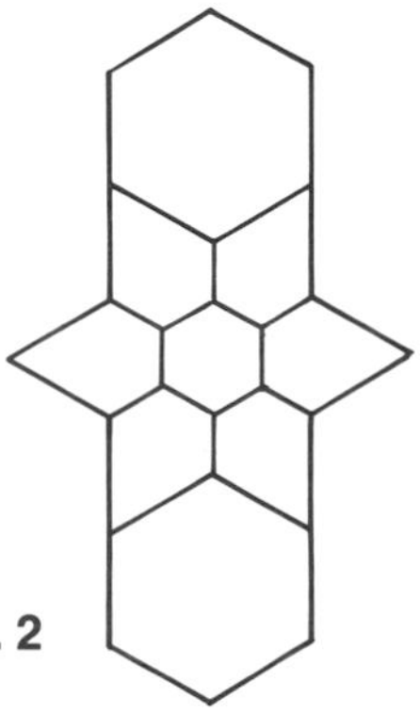

Fig. 2

B. Joining units:

Step 1. Join as shown (Fig. 3).

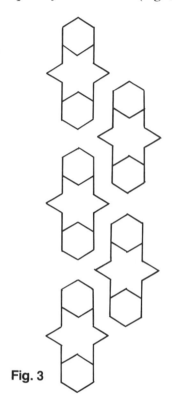

Fig. 3

Step 2. Trim edges even (Fig. 4).

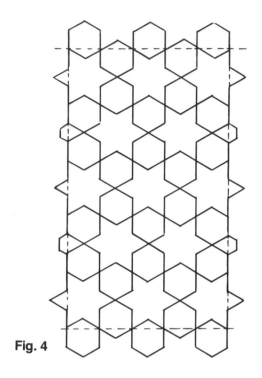

Fig. 4

C. Add borders.

Finishing

A. Quilt as desired.
B. Turn $1\frac{1}{2}''$ of outer border to back of quilt. Turn under $\frac{1}{2}''$. Pin and stitch.

Yardages

Fabrics	CR	TW	D	Q	K	SQ	OB
1 (A)	$1\frac{3}{4}$	3	4	4	$4\frac{3}{4}$	$2\frac{1}{8}$	$1\frac{3}{4}$
2 (B)	$\frac{3}{8}$	$\frac{5}{8}$	$\frac{7}{8}$	$\frac{7}{8}$	1	$\frac{1}{2}$	$\frac{3}{8}$
3 (C)	$1\frac{1}{2}$	$2\frac{3}{4}$	$3\frac{1}{2}$	$3\frac{1}{2}$	$4\frac{1}{2}$	2	$1\frac{1}{2}$
1st border	$\frac{3}{4}$	$\frac{3}{4}$	$\frac{3}{4}$	$\frac{3}{4}$	$\frac{3}{4}$	$\frac{3}{4}$	$\frac{1}{2}$
2nd border	—	1	$1\frac{1}{4}$	$1\frac{1}{4}$	$1\frac{1}{2}$	1	$\frac{3}{4}$
3rd border	—	$2\frac{1}{2}$	$2\frac{1}{2}$	$3\frac{1}{4}$	$3\frac{3}{4}$	—	$1\frac{3}{4}$
Backing	$2\frac{3}{4}$	$6\frac{1}{4}$	8	8	10	$3\frac{3}{4}$	$3\frac{1}{2}$

Cutting Borders

• To cut length of outer borders, add 6″ to finished sizes of quilt.
• Cut all other borders to finished quilt size.
• Trim as needed.
• All outer borders include 1½″ extra to turn back for finished edge.

Yardage Notes

• All yardages include a small amount for shrinkage and waste.
• Yardages are for pieced borders, to conserve fabric. You may prefer an unpieced border, especially on wider borders. Use the longest side of your finished quilt to determine how many yards to buy.

Options

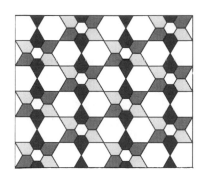
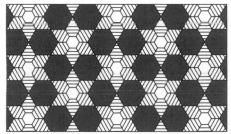
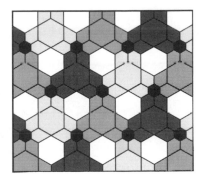

Six-Point Star
Design Page

For quick reference or design-your-own:

1. Copy this page.
2. Trim copy to desired quilt size.
3. Color design.

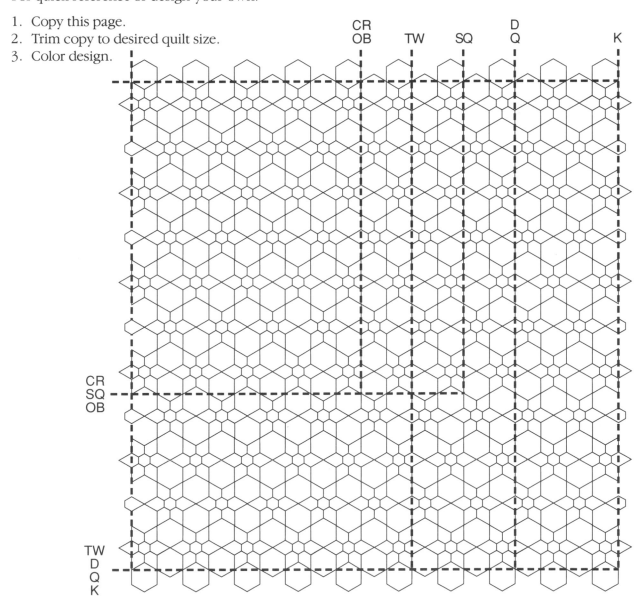

17. WHIRLING CONES
Intermediate

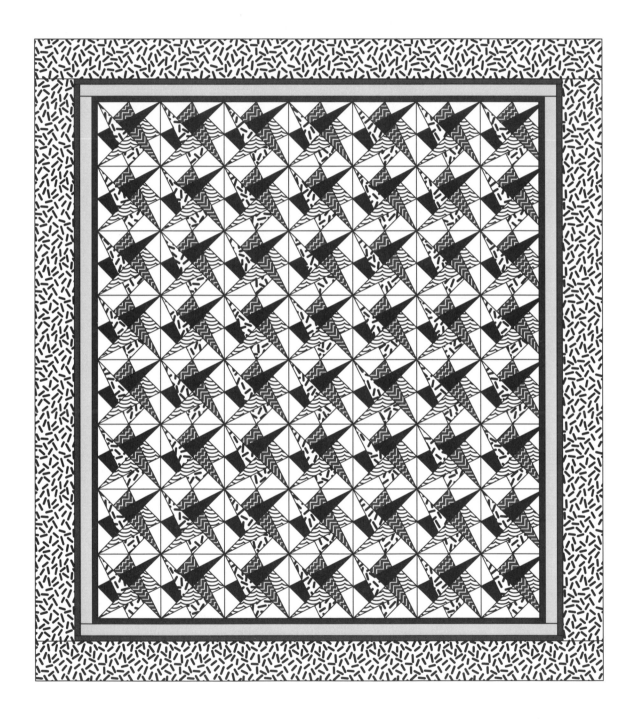

Dimensions (inches)

	CR	TW	D	Q	K	SQ	OB
Finished quilt	50 × 60	72 × 102	84 × 108	86 × 110	108 × 108	64 × 64	54 × 74
Center	40 × 50	50 × 80	60 × 84	60 × 84	84 × 84	50 × 50	40 × 60
1st border	1½	1½	1½	1½	1½	2	2
2nd border	3½	3	3	4	3	5	5
3rd border	—	1½	1½	1½	1½	—	—
4th border	—	5	6	6	6	—	—

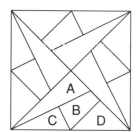

To Speed-Cut:
    A,C. Odd-shaped triangle, 90°
    B. Unusual shape, 90°
    D. Triangle, 45°

Cutting Instructions

	CR	TW	D	Q	K	SQ	OB
Size of square	10″	10″	12″	12″	12″	10″	10″
Number needed							
A (fabrics 1 through 4, each)	20	40	35	35	49	25	24
B (fabrics 1 through 4, each)	20	40	35	35	49	25	24
C (fabric 5)	80	160	140	140	196	100	96
D (fabric 5)	80	160	140	140	196	100	96
Cut widths							
Cut 1st border	2″	2″	2″	2″	2″	2½″	2½″
Cut 2nd border	5½″	3½″	3½″	4½″	3½″	7″	7″
Cut 3rd border	—	2″	2″	2″	2″	—	—
Cut 4th border	—	7″	8″	8″	8″	—	—

General Information

	CR	TW	D	Q	K	SQ	OB
Blocks Across	4	5	5	5	7	5	4
Blocks Down	5	8	7	7	7	5	6
Total	20	40	35	35	49	25	24

Whirling Cones
Instructions

Cutting Notes: All fabric must be stacked *right side up.*

Piecing

A. Piecing blocks:

Step 1. Sew B and C pieces (Fig. 1).

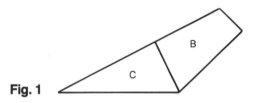

Fig. 1

Step 2. Add D pieces (Fig. 2).

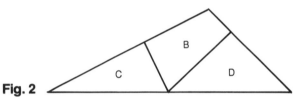

Fig. 2

Step 3. Add A pieces (Fig. 3).

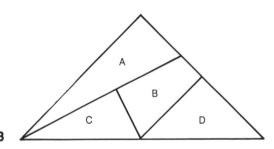

Fig. 3

Step 4. Sew 4 triangle units together to form block (Fig. 4).

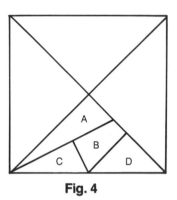

Fig. 4

B. Sew blocks together.

C. Add borders.

Finishing

A. Quilt as desired.

B. Turn 1¹⁄₂″ of outer border to back of quilt. Turn under ¹⁄₂″. Pin and stitch.

Yardages

Fabrics	CR	TW	D	Q	K	SQ	OB
1 (cones A, B)	3/4	1 3/8	1 1/8	1 1/8	1 3/4	7/8	1
2 (cones A, B)	3/4	1 3/8	1 1/8	1 1/8	1 3/4	7/8	1
3 (cones A, B)	3/4	1 3/8	1 1/8	1 1/8	1 3/4	7/8	1
4 (cones A, B)	3/4	1 3/8	1 1/8	1 1/8	1 3/4	7/8	1
5 (background C, D)	1 3/4	3 1/2	2 3/4	2 3/4	3 7/8	2 1/8	1 7/8
1st border	1/2	3/4	3/4	3/4	3/4	3/4	3/4
2nd border	1 1/4	1	1 1/4	1 1/2	1 1/2	1 3/4	1 3/4
3rd border	—	3/4	3	3/4	3/4	—	—
4th border	—	2	2 1/2	2 1/2	3	—	—
Backing	3 1/4	6 3/4	8 1/2	8 1/2	10 1/4	4	3 3/4

Cutting Borders

• To cut length of outer borders, add 6" to finished sizes of quilt.
• Cut all other borders to finished quilt size.
• Trim as needed.
• All outer borders include 1 1/2" extra to turn back for finished edge.

Yardage Notes

• All yardages include a small amount for shrinkage and waste.
• Yardages are for pieced borders, to conserve fabric. You may prefer an unpieced border, especially on wider borders. Use the longest side of your finished quilt to determine how many yards to buy.

Options

Whirling Cones
Design Page

For quick reference or design-your-own:

1. Copy this page.
2. Trim copy to desired quilt size.
3. Color design.

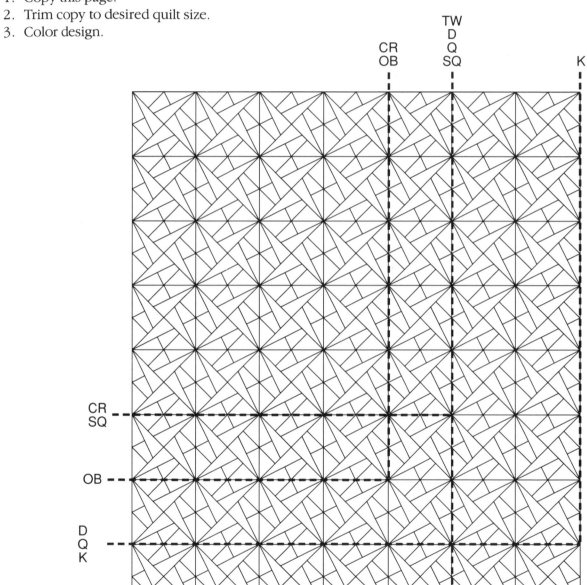

18. FLOWER BASKET
Advanced

Dimensions (inches)

	CR	TW	D	Q	K	SQ	OB
Finished quilt	46 × 64	76 × 104	90 × 104	92 × 106	110 × 110	66 × 66	59 × 73
Center	38 × 56	56 × 84	70 × 84	70 × 84	84 × 84	56 × 56	41 × 55
1st border	3	1½	1½	1½	1½	1	1½
2nd border	—	3	3	3	3	3	2½
3rd border	—	4½	4½	5½	1½	—	4
4th border	—	—	—	—	6	—	—

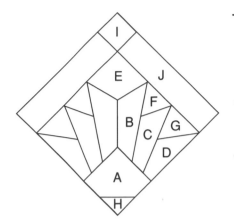

Cut blocks for:
Side triangles, 12″ × 12″
Corner triangles, 9″ × 9″

To Speed Cut:
A. Lop-eared square
B,C,D,E. Unusual shapes, 60°
F,G. Triangle, 60°
H. Triangle, 45°
I. Square
J. Rectangle

Cutting Instructions

	CR	TW	D	Q	K	SQ	OB
Number needed							
A (fabric 1)	18	39	50	50	61	25	18
B (fabric 2)*	36	78	100	100	122	50	36
C (fabric 3)*	36	78	100	100	122	50	36
D (fabric 4)*	36	78	100	100	122	50	36
E, H (each, fabric 6)	18	39	50	50	61	25	18
F, G (each, fabric 6)*	36	78	100	100	122	50	36
I (fabric 5)	20	39	50	50	61	28	20
J (fabric 7)	36	78	100	100	122	50	36
Edge triangles (fabric 8)	10	16	18	18	20	12	10
Corner triangles (fabric 8)	4	4	4	4	4	4	4
Cut widths							
Cut 1st border	5″	2″	2″	2″	2″	1½″	2″
Cut 2nd border	—	3½″	3½″	3½″	3½″	5″	3″
Cut 3rd border	—	6½″	6½″	7½″	2″	—	6″
Cut 4th border	—	—	—	—	8″	—	—

General Information

	CR	TW	D	Q	K	SQ	OB
Blocks Across	3	4	5	5	6	4	3
Blocks Down	4	6	6	6	6	4	4
Total	18	39	50	50	61	25	18

*Reverse half of pieces B, C, D, F, G.

Flower Basket Instructions

Cutting Notes: *So many shapes in this block are mirror images that, just to be safe, stack all the fabrics with like sides together!*

Piecing

A. Piecing blocks:
   Step 1. Join flower pieces (Fig. 1).

   Note: *It is very easy to join the wrong edge of piece G. If sewn correctly, the long edges will both be straight (Fig. 2).*

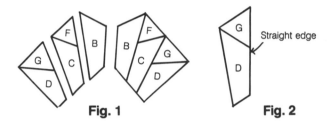

Fig. 1   **Fig. 2**

Straight edge

   Step 2. Join remaining units (Fig. 3).
   Step 3. Insert A and E (Fig. 4).

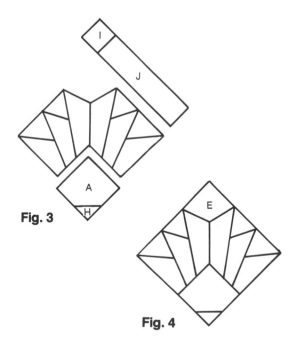

Fig. 3

Fig. 4

Step 4. Add lattice units (Fig. 5).

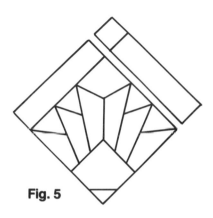

Fig. 5

B. Joining blocks and triangles:

   Step 1. Join units to form strips (Fig. 6).

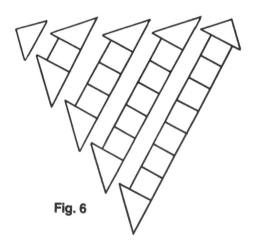

Fig. 6

   Step 2. Join strips.
C. Add borders.

Finishing

A. Quilt as desired.
B. Turn 1½" of outer border to back of quilt. Turn under ½". Pin and stitch.

Yardages

Fabrics	CR	TW	D	Q	K	SQ	OB
1 (A)	1/2	1/2	3/4	3/4	7/8	1/2	1/2
2 (B)	1/2	7/8	1 1/8	1 1/8	1 3/8	3/4	1/2
3 (C)	3/8	3/4	1	1	1 1/4	5/8	3/8
4 (D)	3/8	3/4	7/8	7/8	1 1/8	1/2	3/8
5 (I)	1/8	1/4	1/4	1/4	3/8	1/4	1/8
6 (E, F, G, H)	1	1 3/4	2	2	2 1/4	1 1/4	1
7 (J)	3/4	1 1/2	2 1/4	2 1/4	2 1/2	1	3/4
8 (triangles)	3/4	1 1/4	1 1/4	1 1/2	1 3/4	1	3/4
1st border	1 1/4	3/4	3/4	3/4	3/4	1/2	1/2
2nd border	—	1	1 1/4	1 1/4	1 1/2	1 1/4	3/4
3rd border	—	1 3/4	2	2 1/4	3/4	—	1 1/2
4th border	—	—	—	—	3	—	—
Backing	3 1/4	6 3/4	8 1/2	8 1/2	10 1/4	4	3 3/4

Cutting Borders

- To cut length of outer borders, add 6″ to finished sizes of quilt.
- Cut all other borders to finished quilt size.
- Trim as needed.
- All outer borders include 1 1/2″ extra to turn back for finished edge.

Yardage Notes

- All yardages include a small amount for shrinkage and waste.
- Yardages are for pieced borders, to conserve fabric. You may prefer an unpieced border, especially on wider borders. Use the longest side of your finished quilt to determine how many yards to buy.

Options

Flower Basket
Design Page

For quick reference or design-your-own:

1. Copy this page.
2. Trim copy to desired quilt size.
3. Color design.

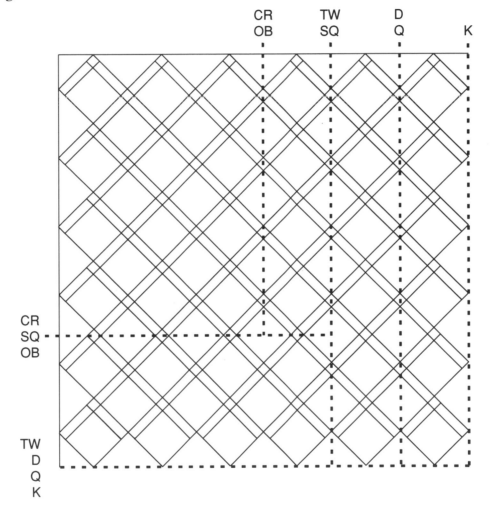

19. DOUBLE WEDDING RING
Advanced

Dimensions (inches)

	CR	TW	D	Q	K	SQ	OB
Finished quilt	41 × 63	74 × 96	86 × 96	86 × 108	108 × 108	63 × 63	63 × 74

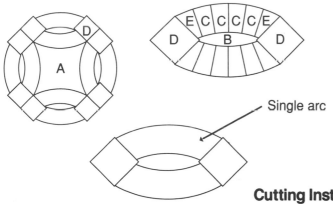

To Speed Cut:
  B. Crescent
  C,E. Arc pieces
  D. Square

Single arc

Cutting Instructions

	CR	TW	D	Q	K	SQ	OB
Number needed							
A (fabric 1)	15	48	56	63	81	25	30
B (fabric 1)	38	110	127	142	180	60	71
C (fabrics 2 through 5, each)	76	220	254	284	360	120	142
E (fabrics 6 and 7, each)	76	220	254	284	360	120	142
D (fabrics 8 and 9, each)	48	126	144	160	200	72	84
Binding	Cut bias strip 2½″ wide						
Single arc*	76	220	254	284	360	120	142

General Information

	CR	TW	D	Q	K	SQ	OB
Rings Across	3	6	7	7	9	5	5
Rings Down	5	8	8	9	9	5	6
Total	15	48	56	63	81	25	30

*Optional: replaces C and E pieces

Double Wedding Ring
Instructions

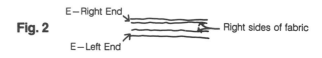

Cutting Notes: *Cut crescents and centers as shown (Fig. 1). Stack fabric right side up for E pieces on left end of arc and wrong side up for those on the right end of arc (Fig. 2).*

Fig. 1

Fig. 2

E—Right End

Right sides of fabric

E—Left End

Piecing

A. Piecing units:

Step 1. Sew arc pieces as shown (short arcs); (Fig. 3).

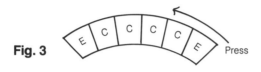

Fig. 3

Step 2. Add corner squares to both ends of half the arc units (long arcs); (Fig. 4).

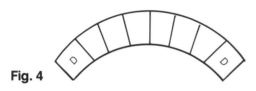

Fig. 4

Step 3. Pin short arc to crescent piece at center point (Fig. 5). With crescent on top, stitch to pin (Fig. 6). With needle in fabric, match ends of seam. Stitch remainder of seam (Fig. 7).

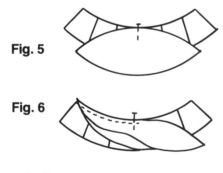

Fig. 5

Fig. 6

Fig. 7

Step 4. Pin long arc to crescent/arc unit. Pin at center point and corner seams (Fig. 8). Stitch as in Step 3 (Fig. 9).

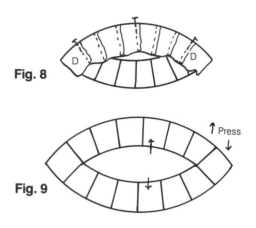

Fig. 8

Fig. 9

B. Joining the units:

Note: *Prepare a test double wedding ring, using a basting stitch. If this unit lies flat, proceed with the quilt. If there is excess fabric in the center piece, you'll want to make adjustments. Try shortening the "arms" of the center piece. Then recut your template to match the adjustment (Fig. 10).*

Fig. 10

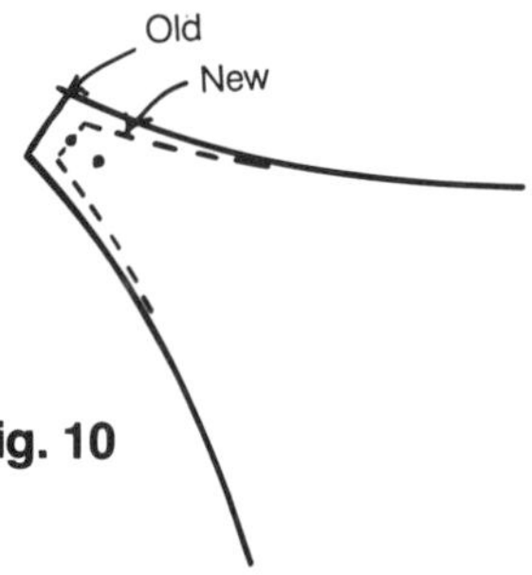

Step 1. Pin center piece to crescent unit. Pin at center point and corner seams (Fig. 11). Stitch *only* to these corner seams. Backstitch lightly.

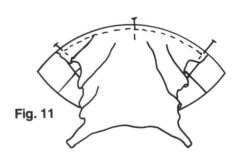

Fig. 11

Step 2. Join crescent unit to adjacent side of center piece (Fig. 12).

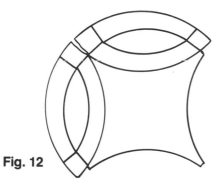

Fig. 12

Step 3. Join corner blocks, stitching from inner ring to outer edge (Fig. 13).

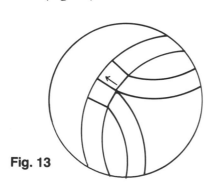

Fig. 13

Step 4. Join remaining crescents/center units as shown in layout (Fig. 14).

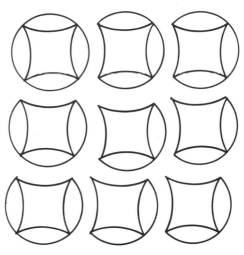

Fig. 14

Finishing

A. Quilt as desired.

B. Cut bias binding 2¹/₂″ wide. Bind, following curved edges.

Yardages

Fabrics	CR	TW	D	Q	K	SQ	OB
1 (A and B)	2¹/₄	5¹/₄	6¹/₄	6³/₄	8¹/₂	3¹/₄	4
2 through 5, each (C)	³/₄	1¹/₂	1¹/₂	1³/₄	2¹/₂	⁷/₈	1
6 and 7, each (E)	³/₄	1¹/₂	1¹/₂	1³/₄	2¹/₂	⁷/₈	1
8 and 9, each (D)	³/₈	³/₄	⁷/₈	⁷/₈	1¹/₂	¹/₂	⁵/₈
Binding	2¹/₈	3¹/₈	3¹/₄	3¹/₂	5	2³/₈	2¹/₂
Backing	2	6	6³/₄	7³/₄	10¹/₂	4	4
Single arc*	2¹/₄	5¹/₂	6³/₈	7¹/₈	9	3¹/₂	3⁷/₈

*Optional: replaces C and E pieces.

Yardage Notes

• All yardages include a small amount for shrinkage and waste.

Options

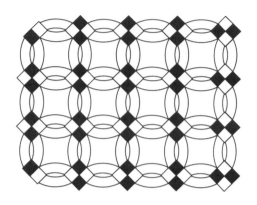

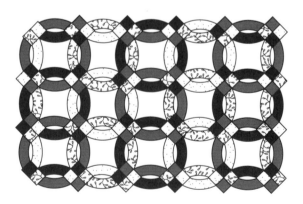

Double Wedding Ring
Design Page

For quick reference or design-your-own:

1. Copy this page.
2. Trim copy to desired quilt size.
3. Color design.

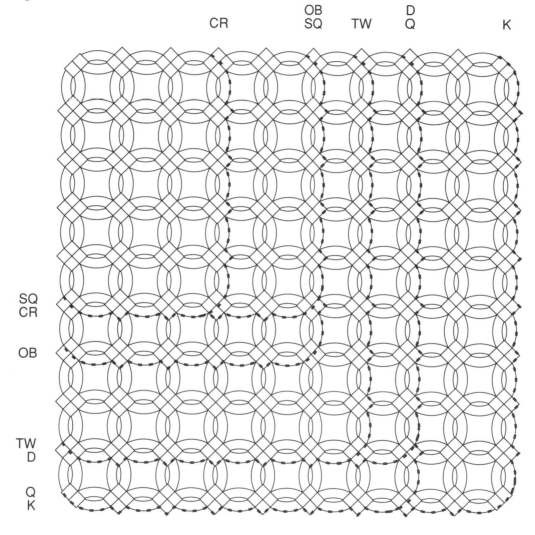

20. NOSEGAY
Advanced

Dimensions (inches)

	CR	TW	D	Q	K	SQ	OB
Finished quilt	47 × 64	70 × 104	87 × 104	91 × 108	110 × 110	66 × 66	58 × 75
Center	35 × 52	52 × 86	69 × 86	69 × 86	86 × 86	52 × 52	52 × 69
1st border	2	1½	1½	1½	1½	2	3
2nd border	4	3	3	3	3	5	—
3rd border	—	4½	4½	1½	1½	—	—
4th border	—	—	—	5	6	—	—

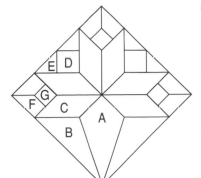

Cut squares for:
Edge triangles, 14″ × 14″
Corner triangles, 10½″ × 10½″

To Speed Cut:
A,B. Odd-shape triangle, 45°
C. Long diamond, 45°
D,G. Square
E. Triangle, 45°
F. Shoe, 45°

Cutting Instructions

	CR	TW	D	Q	K	SQ	OB
Number needed							
A (fabric 1)	8	23	32	32	41	13	18
C (fabric 2, half reversed)	48	138	192	192	246	78	108
D (fabric 3)	16	46	64	64	82	26	36
G (fabric 4)	24	69	96	96	123	39	54
B (fabric 5, half reversed)	16	46	64	64	82	26	36
F (fabric 5, half reversed)	48	138	192	192	246	78	108
E (fabric 5)	32	92	128	128	164	52	72
Side triangles (fabric 6)	6	12	14	14	16	8	10
Corner triangles (fabric 6)	4	4	4	4	4	4	4
Cut widths							
Cut 1st border	2½″	2″	2″	2″	2″	2½″	5″
Cut 2nd border	6″	3½″	3½″	3½″	3½″	7″	—
Cut 3rd border	—	6½″	6½″	2″	2″	—	—
Cut 4th border	—	—	—	7″	8″	—	—

General Information

	CR	TW	D	Q	K	SQ	OB
Blocks Across	2	3	4	4	5	3	3
Blocks Down	3	5	5	5	5	3	4
Total	8	23	32	32	41	13	18

Nosegay
Instructions

Cutting Notes: *So many shapes in this block are mirror images that, just to be safe, stack all the fabrics with like sides together.*

Piecing

A. Piecing blocks:
   Step 1. Piece leaf units (Fig. 1).

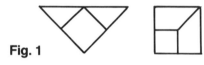

Fig. 1

   Step 2. Piece petal and cone units (Figs. 2 and 3).

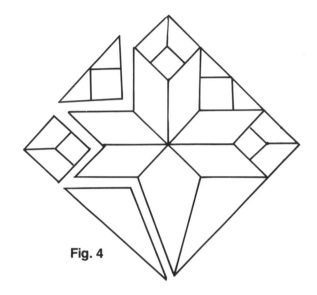

Fig. 4

B. Joining blocks and triangles:

   Step 1. Join units to form strips (Fig. 5).

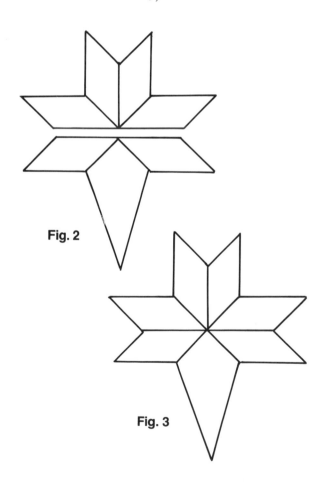

Fig. 2

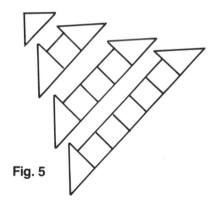

Fig. 5

   Step 2. Join strips (Fig. 6).

Fig. 3

   Step 3. Add leaf units and B pieces (Fig. 4).

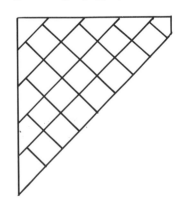

Fig. 6

C. Add borders.

Finishing

A. Quilt as desired.

B. Turn 1½″ of outer border to back of quilt. Turn under ½″. Pin and stitch.

Yardages

Fabrics	CR	TW	D	Q	K	SQ	OB
1 (A)	³/₈	³/₄	1	1	1¼	½	⁵/₈
2 (C)	⁷/₈	2¼	3¼	3¼	4	1¼	1³/₄
3 (D)	½	³/₈	½	½	½	¼	³/₈
4 (G)	⅛	¼	³/₈	³/₈	½	¼	¼
5 (B, E, F)	1	2	2³/₄	2³/₄	3³/₈	1³/₈	1³/₄
6 (triangles)	1	1½	1³/₄	1³/₄	1³/₄	1	1½
1st border	³/₄	³/₄	³/₄	³/₄	³/₄	³/₄	1¼
2nd border	1½	1	1¼	1¼	1½	1³/₄	—
3rd border	—	1³/₄	2	³/₄	³/₄	—	—
4th border	—	—	—	2¼	3	—	—
Backing	3	6¼	8	8	10¼	4	3½

Cutting Borders

- To cut length of outer borders, add 6″ to finished sizes of quilt.
- Cut all other borders to finished quilt size.
- Trim as needed.
- All outer borders include 1½″ extra to turn back for finished edge.

Yardage Notes

- All yardages include a small amount for shrinkage and waste.
- Yardages are for pieced borders, to conserve fabric. You may prefer an unpieced border, especially on wider borders. Use the longest side of your finished quilt to determine how many yards to buy.

Options

Nosegay
Design Page

For quick reference or design-your-own:

1. Copy this page.
2. Trim copy to desired quilt size.
3. Color design.

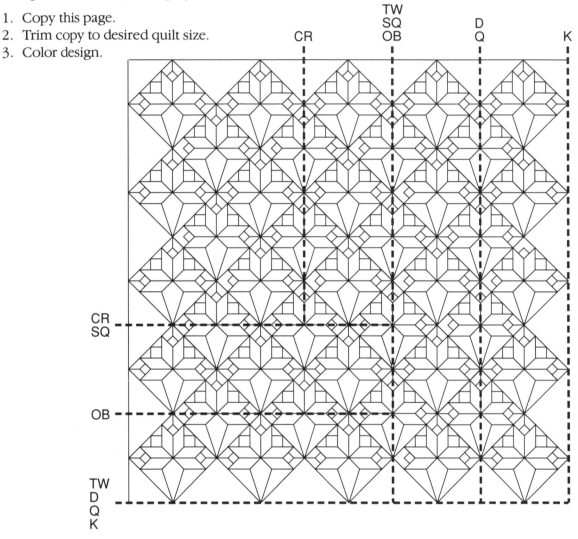

Now that you've learned my Speedy System, you can apply the knowledge to all your quilts! No longer will you look at a gorgeous quilt pattern and think, "I'd love to make that, but the thought of drawing around all those little pieces is just too depressing. Forget it." Now you'll grab my book, thumb through it till you find the methods for each of those pieces, and merrily dive right in!

Appendix A

YARDAGE CHARTS, BACKING, AND BORDERS

The following pages are information for your use if you'd like to design your own quilt.

Using the design page of the quilt you want to make plus the Play-Plan, you can easily determine the number of pieces you need of each template.

The yardage page will tell you how many pieces you can cut from 1/4-, 1/2- and 1-yard cuts of fabric.

The border pages are suggested borders only. Create your own, too. They're a lot of fun. To find yardages for borders, look through the 20 Quilts section for a similar border. For example, if you're cutting a border 4 1/2" wide for a king size quilt, you'll find one in the second border of Tumbling Blocks. It takes 1 3/4 yards.

Yardage Chart for Templates for Design-Your-Own Use

Template	Number of Pieces from: 1/4 yard	1/2 yard	1 yard
All Tied Up			
A	9	27	63
B	50	100	220
C	42	112	224
D	48	96	192
Always Friends			
A	8	32	64
Bow Tie			
A	24	48	108
B	54	126	252
Clamshell			
A	26	52	130
Double Wedding Ring			
A	—	4	12
B	10	30	60
C	40	100	220
D	54	126	252
E	40	100	220
Single Arc	8	20	44
Dresden Plate			
A	12	36	72
B	24	48	108
Drunkards Path			
3" A	24	48	108
B	48	96	192
4" A	9	27	63
B	26	65	143
5" A	7	14	35
B	22	44	99
Fan			
A	16	32	64
B	24	48	120
Flower Basket			
A	10	40	80
B	21	42	98
C	24	48	104

Template	Number of Pieces from: 1/4 yard	1/2 yard	1 yard
Flower Basket (cont.)			
D	27	54	108
E	24	48	108
F	46	115	253
G	40	100	220
H	36	192	384
I	48	96	192
J	12	24	48
Grandmother's Flower Garden			
A	22	55	121
Indian Star			
A	16	48	96
B	39	104	208
C	30	80	160
Little Dahlia			
A	14	28	70
B	28	70	140
Magnolias			
A	9	27	63
B	28	70	154
C	48	96	192
D	80	160	352
E	140	280	588
Nighttime			
A	13	39	91
B	28	63	126
C	68	153	306
Nosegay			
A	6	18	36
B	12	24	48
C	14	35	77
D	32	80	176
E	48	112	224
F	26	104	208
G	63	168	336

Template	Number of Pieces from: 1/4 yard	1/2 yard	1 yard
Peacock			
A	6	12	30
B	57	133	266
C	36	84	168
Six-Point Star			
A	7	21	42
B	24	60	132
C	24	60	132
Tumbling Blocks			
A	42	84	182
B	30	70	140
C	52	117	234
Texas Trellis			
A	30	60	130
B	75	150	325
Whirling Cones			
10" A	16	40	88
B	20	50	110
C	24	72	144
D	16	48	112
12" A	16	32	72
B	16	32	80
C	24	48	108
D	14	42	84
Squares			
14"	—	2	4
12 1/2"	—	3	6
12"	—	3	6
10 1/2"	—	3	9
9"	—	4	12
6 1/2"	6	12	30

Yardage and Piecing Guide for Backing

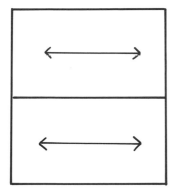

Crib: 3¼ yards.
Oblong tablecloth:
  3¾ yards.

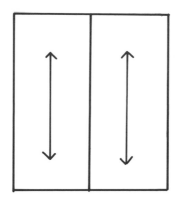

Twin: 6¾ yards.
Square tablecloth:
  4 yards.

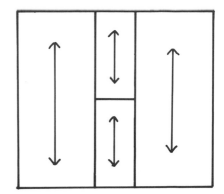

Double: 8½ yards.
Queen: 8½ yards.

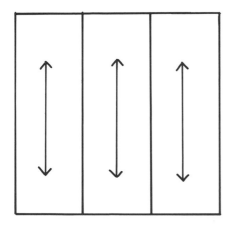

King: 10¼ yards.

Yardage includes small amount for shrinkage and waste.
Arrow indicates lengthwise grain of fabric.

Borders

measurements indicate finished widths, from quilt edge the finished edge

15″ Border
1st—2″
2nd—4″
3rd—2″
4th—7″

14″ Border
1st—2″
2nd—4″
3rd—2″
4th—6″

13″ Border
1st—1½″
2nd—4″
3rd—1½″
4th—6″

12″ Border
1st—1½″
2nd—3″
3rd—1½″
4th—6″

11″ Border
1st—1½″
2nd—3″
3rd—1½″
4th—5″

10″ Border
1st—1½″
2nd—3″
3rd—5½″

9″ Border
1st—1½″
2nd—3″
3rd—4½″

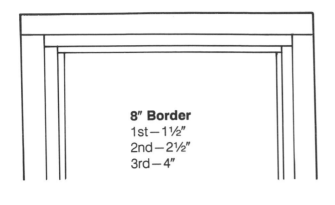

8″ Border
1st—1½″
2nd—2½″
3rd—4″

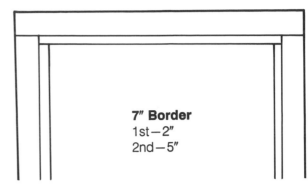

7″ Border
1st—2″
2nd—5″

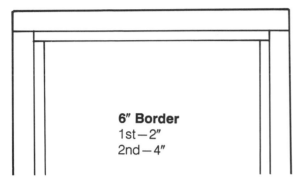

6″ Border
1st—2″
2nd—4″

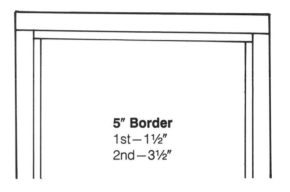

5″ Border
1st—1½″
2nd—3½″

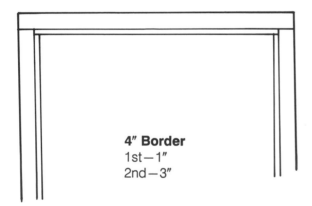

4″ Border
1st—1″
2nd—3″

3″ Border—3″
or
2″ Border—2″

CUT WIDTH OF BORDER STRIPS

Total Border Width	1st Border	2nd Border	3rd Border	4th Border
15″	2½″	4½″	2½″	9″*
14″	2½″	4½″	2½″	8″*
13″	2″	4½″	2″	8″*
12″	2″	3½″	2″	8″*
11″	2″	3½″	2″	7″*
10″	2″	3½″	7½″*	
9″	2″	3½″	6½″*	
8″	2″	3″	6″*	
7″	2½″	7″*		
6″	2½″	6″*		
5″	2″	5½″*		
4″	1½″	5″*		
3″	5″*			
2″	4″*			

*Includes outer border strip. Cut width includes 1¾″ for "binding" turnback.

Appendix B

Full-Size Templates

All Tied Up
(Quilt #9)

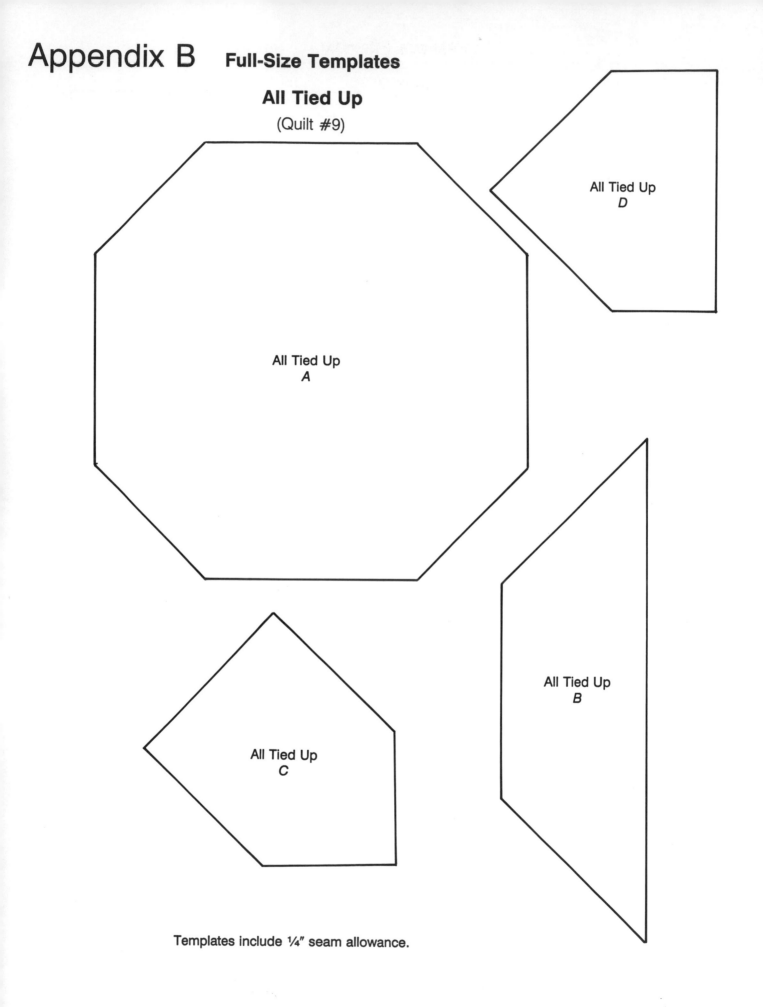

All Tied Up
A

All Tied Up
D

All Tied Up
B

All Tied Up
C

Templates include ¼" seam allowance.

Always Friends

(Quilt #12)

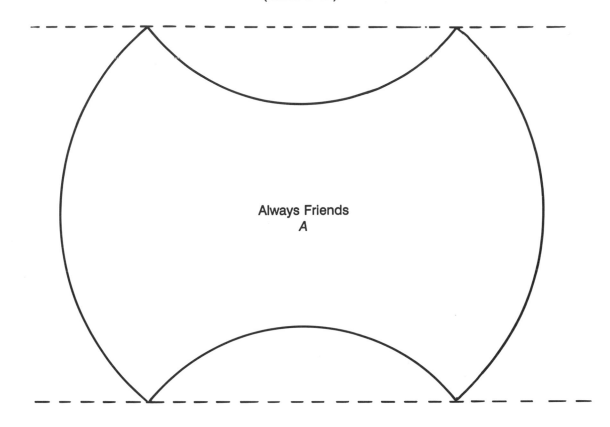

Always Friends
A

Bow Tie

(Quilt #3)

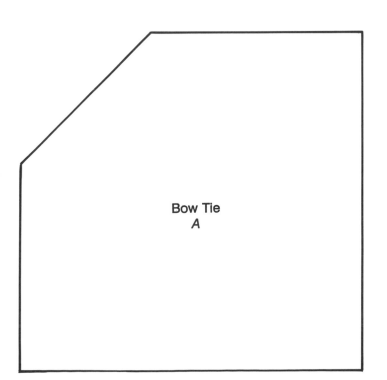

Bow Tie
A

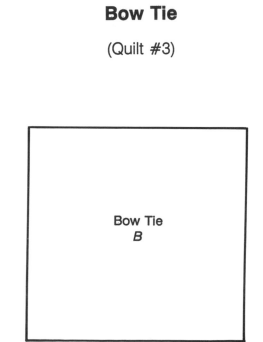

Bow Tie
B

Templates include ¼" seam allowance.

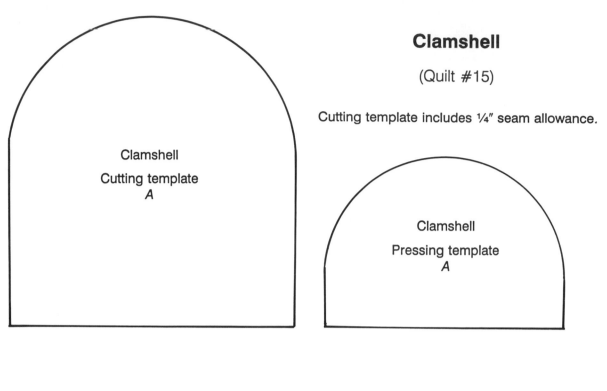

Clamshell

(Quilt #15)

Cutting template includes ¼″ seam allowance.

Clamshell
Cutting template
A

Clamshell
Pressing template
A

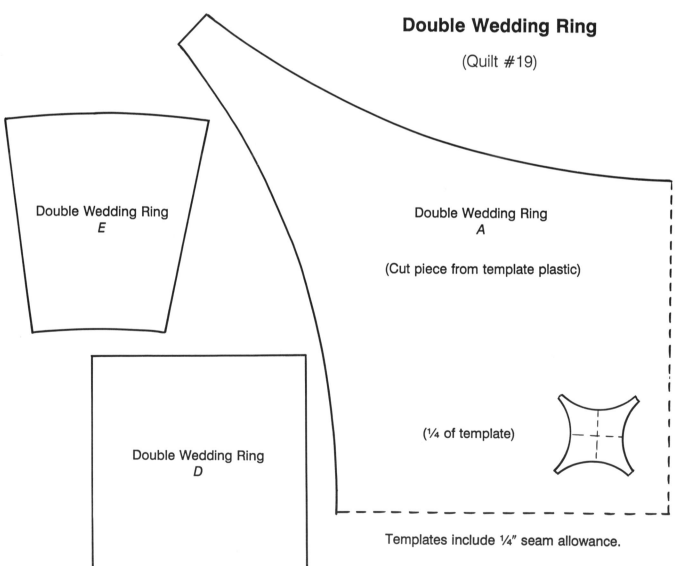

Double Wedding Ring

(Quilt #19)

Double Wedding Ring
E

Double Wedding Ring
A

(Cut piece from template plastic)

(¼ of template)

Double Wedding Ring
D

Templates include ¼″ seam allowance.

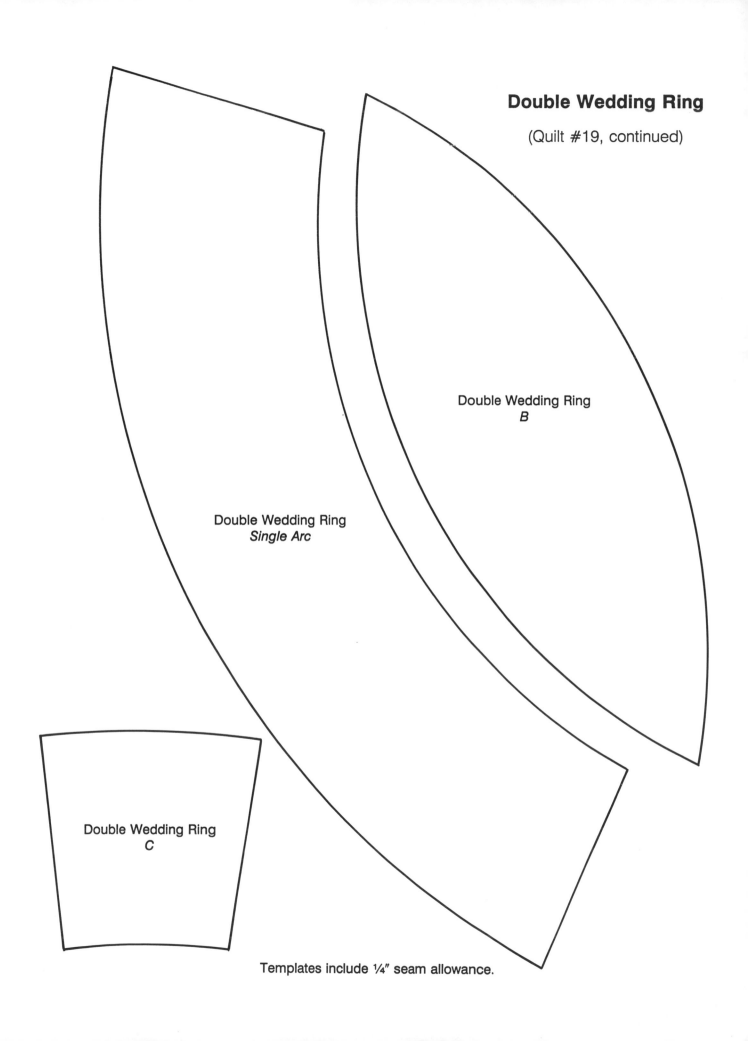

Double Wedding Ring

(Quilt #19, continued)

Double Wedding Ring
B

Double Wedding Ring
Single Arc

Double Wedding Ring
C

Templates include ¼″ seam allowance.

Dresden Plate

(Quilt #2)

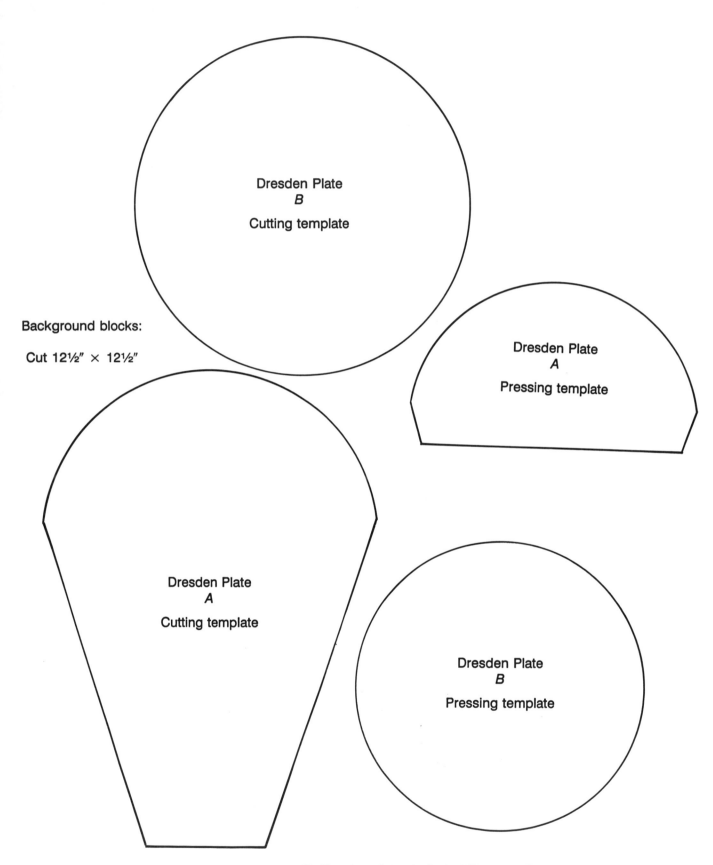

Dresden Plate
B
Cutting template

Dresden Plate
A
Pressing template

Background blocks:

Cut 12½″ × 12½″

Dresden Plate
A
Cutting template

Dresden Plate
B

Pressing template

Cutting templates include ¼″ seam allowance.

Drunkard's Path

(Quilt #10)

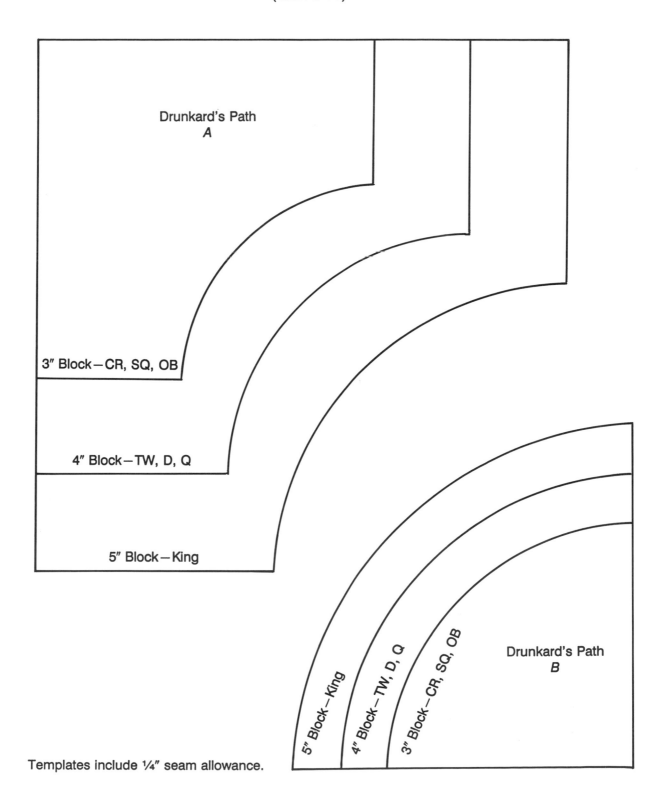

Drunkard's Path
A

3" Block—CR, SQ, OB

4" Block—TW, D, Q

5" Block—King

5" Block—King

4" Block—TW, D, Q

3" Block—CR, SQ, OB

Drunkard's Path
B

Templates include ¼" seam allowance.

Fan

(Quilt #6)

Cut background blocks:

    10½″ × 10½″

Cut squares for:

Edges — 12″ × 12″

Corners — 9″ × 9″

Cut diagonally:

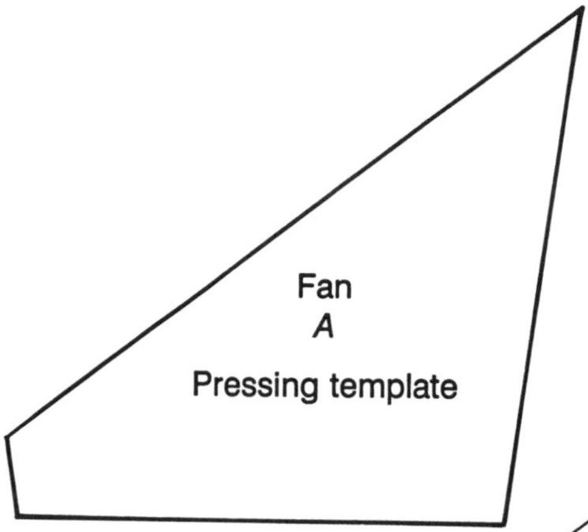

Fan
A
Pressing template

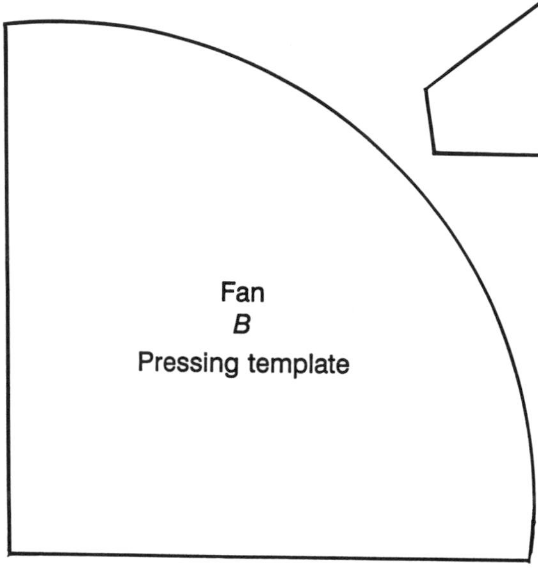

Fan
B
Pressing template

Cutting templates include ¼″ seam allowance.

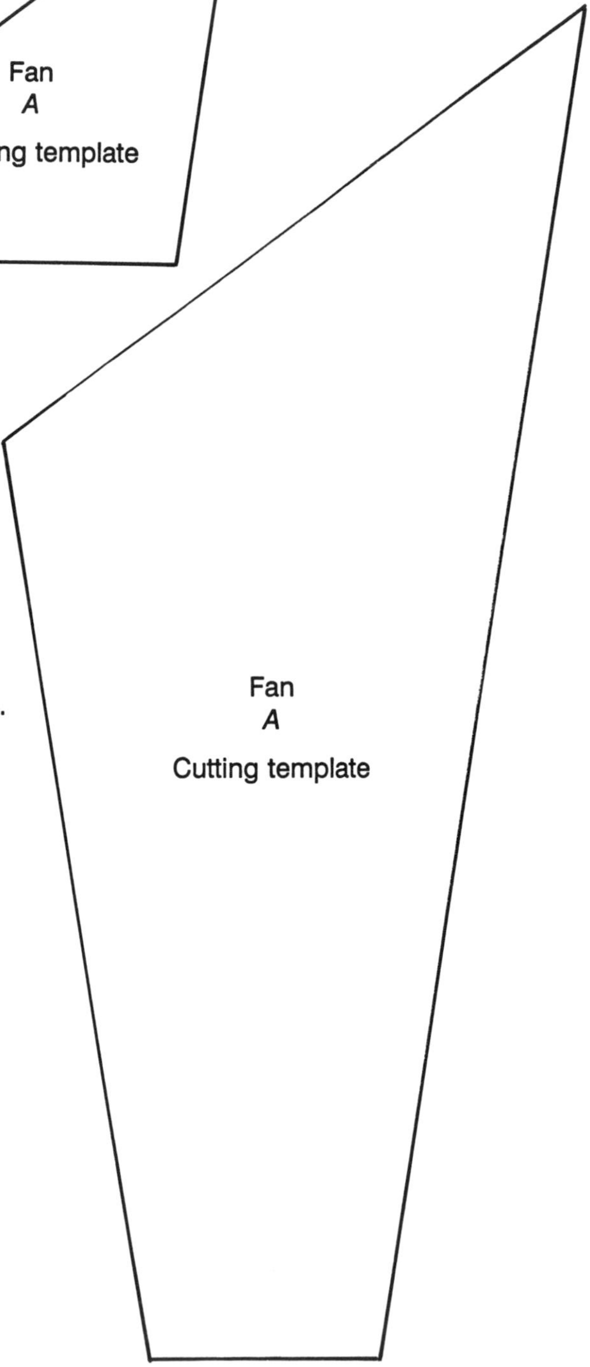

Fan
A
Cutting template

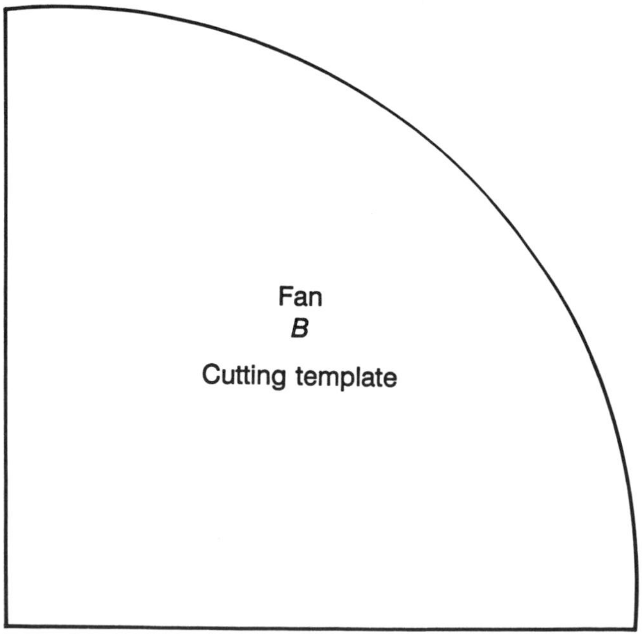

Fan
B
Cutting template

Flower Basket

(Quilt #18)

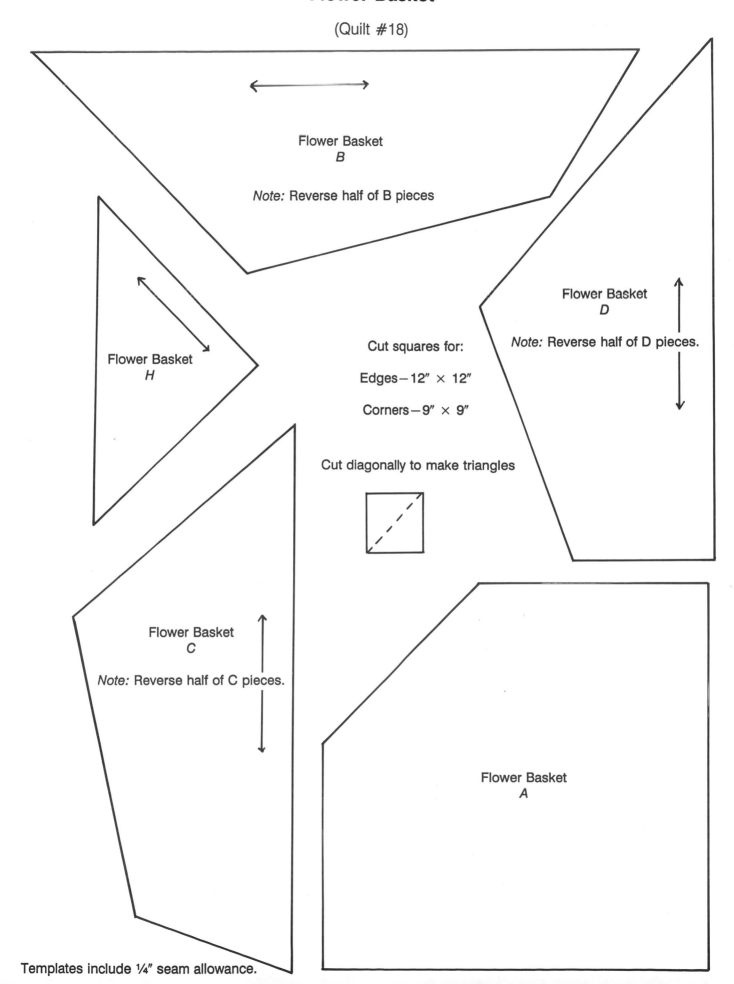

Flower Basket
B

Note: Reverse half of B pieces

Flower Basket
D

Note: Reverse half of D pieces.

Flower Basket
H

Cut squares for:

Edges—12″ × 12″

Corners—9″ × 9″

Cut diagonally to make triangles

Flower Basket
C

Note: Reverse half of C pieces.

Flower Basket
A

Templates include ¼″ seam allowance.

Flower Basket

(Quilt #18, continued)

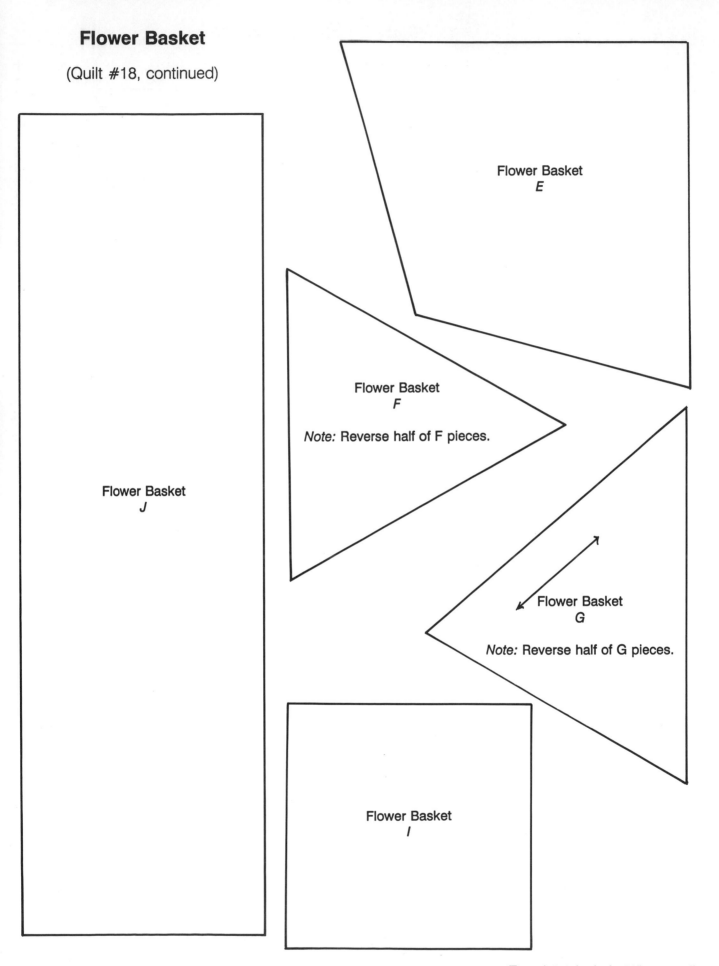

Flower Basket
E

Flower Basket
F

Note: Reverse half of F pieces.

Flower Basket
J

Flower Basket
G

Note: Reverse half of G pieces.

Flower Basket
I

Templates include ¼" seam allowanc

Grandmother's Flower Garden

(Quilt #1)

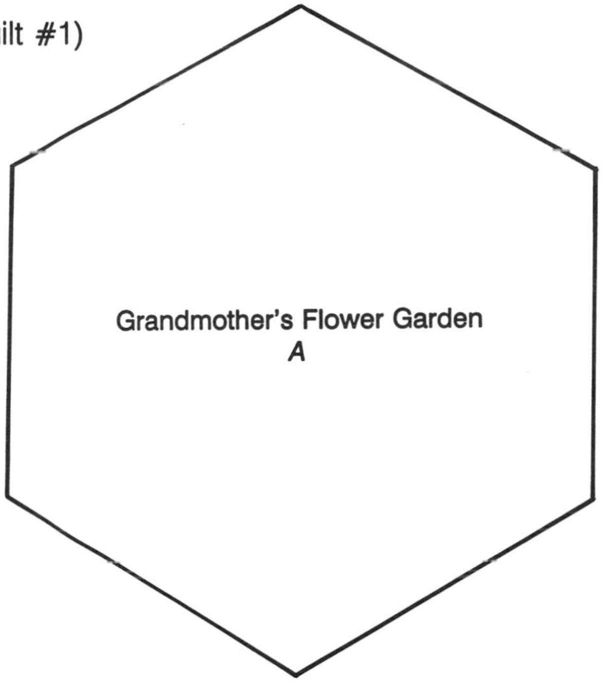

Indian Star

(Quilt #8)

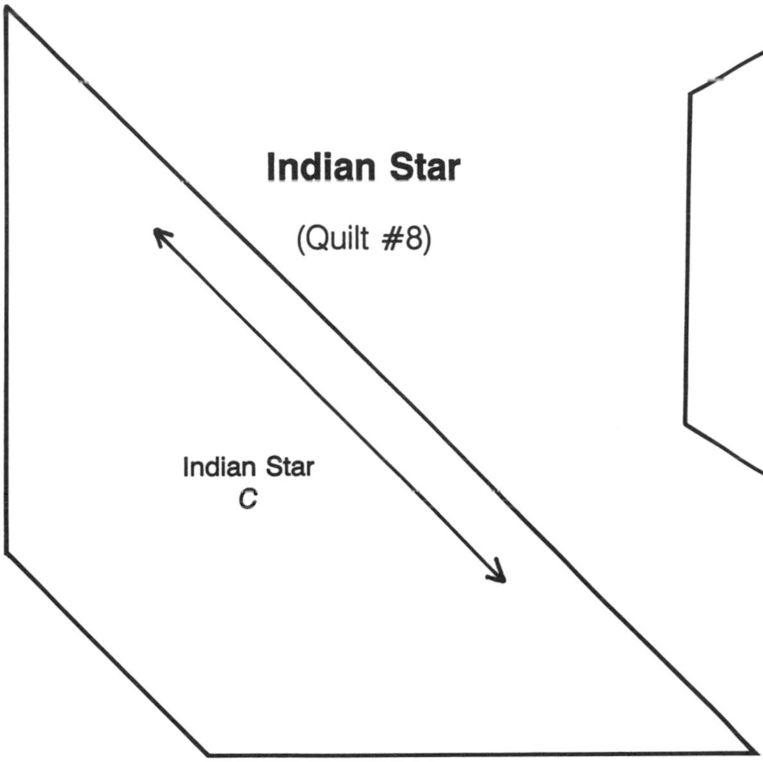

Indian Star
C

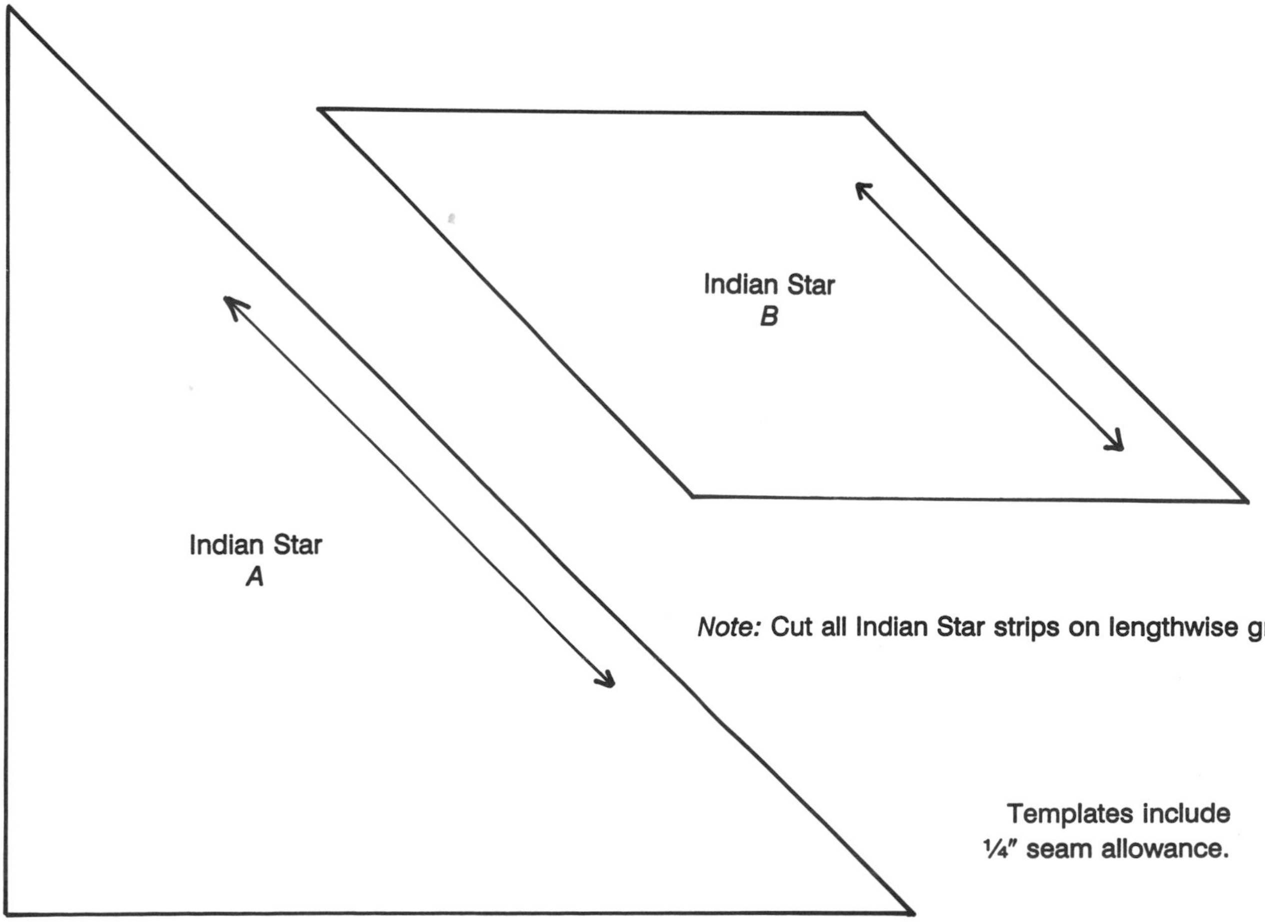

Grandmother's Flower Garden
A

Indian Star
B

Indian Star
A

Note: Cut all Indian Star strips on lengthwise grain.

Templates include
¼" seam allowance.

Little Dahlia

(Quilt #4)

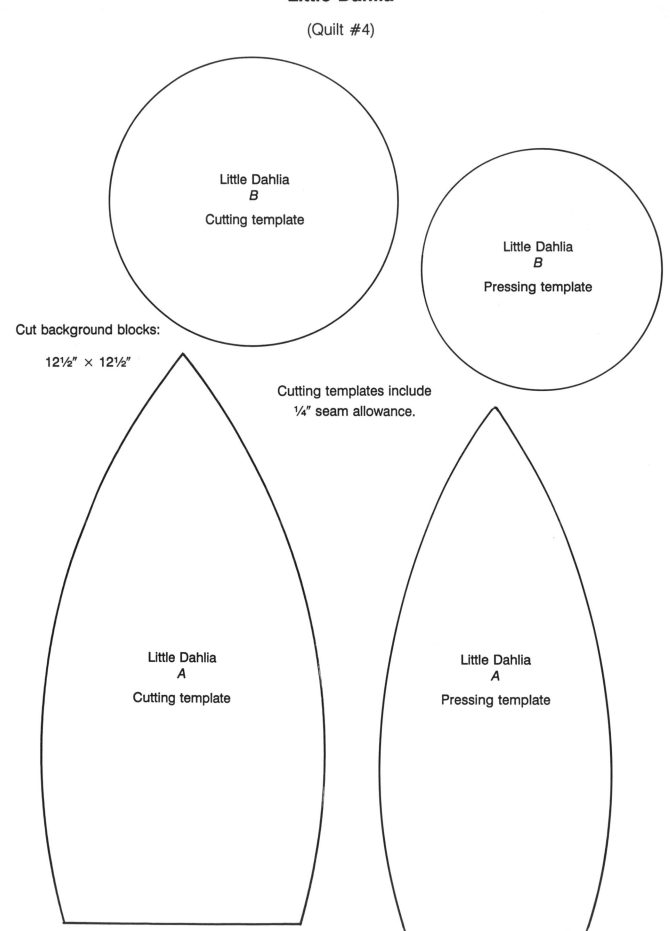

Little Dahlia
B

Cutting template

Little Dahlia
B

Pressing template

Cut background blocks:

12½″ × 12½″

Cutting templates include
¼″ seam allowance.

Little Dahlia
A

Cutting template

Little Dahlia
A

Pressing template

Magnolias

(Quilt #14)

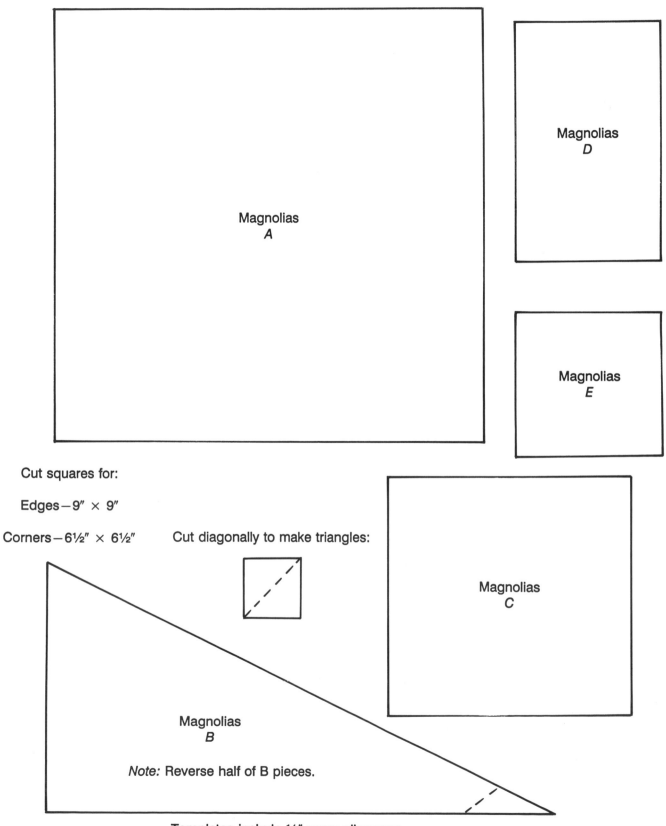

Magnolias
A

Magnolias
D

Magnolias
E

Cut squares for:

Edges — 9″ × 9″

Corners — 6½″ × 6½″

Cut diagonally to make triangles:

Magnolias
C

Magnolias
B

Note: Reverse half of B pieces.

Templates include ¼″ seam allowance.

Nighttime

(Quilt #11)

Cut all Nighttime strips on lengthwise grain.

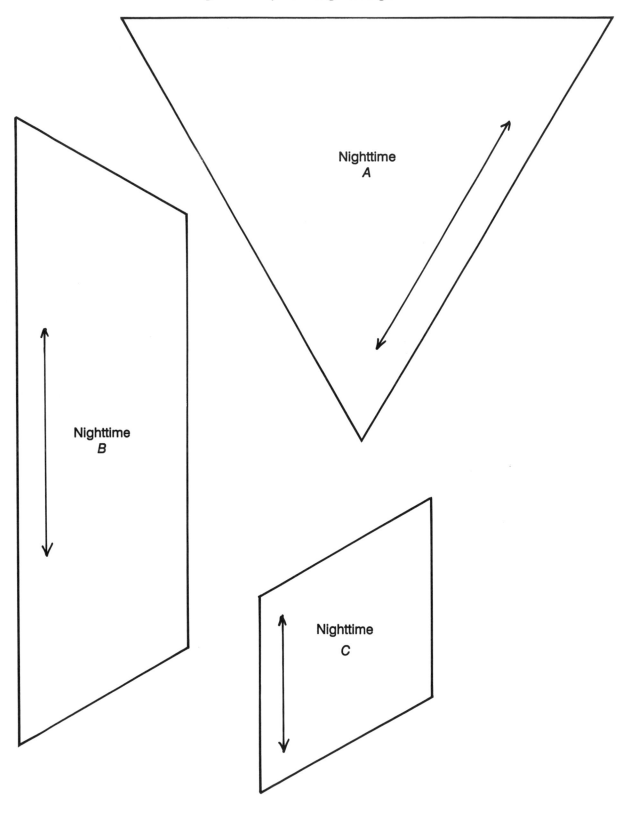

Templates include ¼" seam allowance.

Nosegay

(Quilt #20)

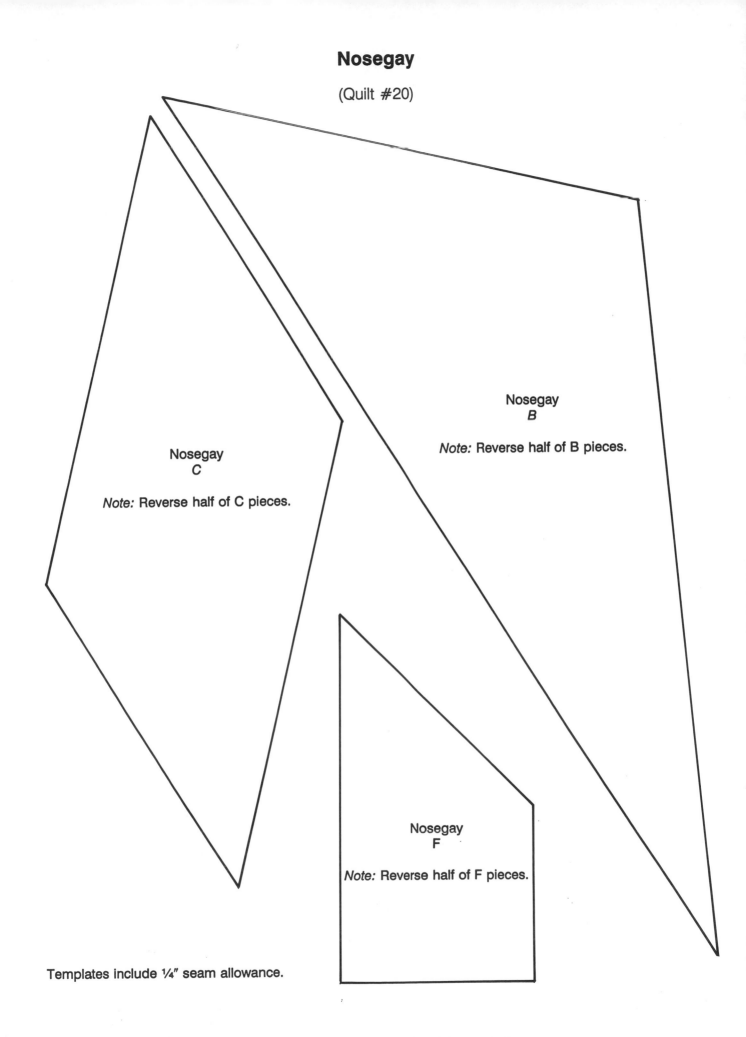

Nosegay
C

Note: Reverse half of C pieces.

Nosegay
B

Note: Reverse half of B pieces.

Nosegay
F

Note: Reverse half of F pieces.

Templates include ¼″ seam allowance.

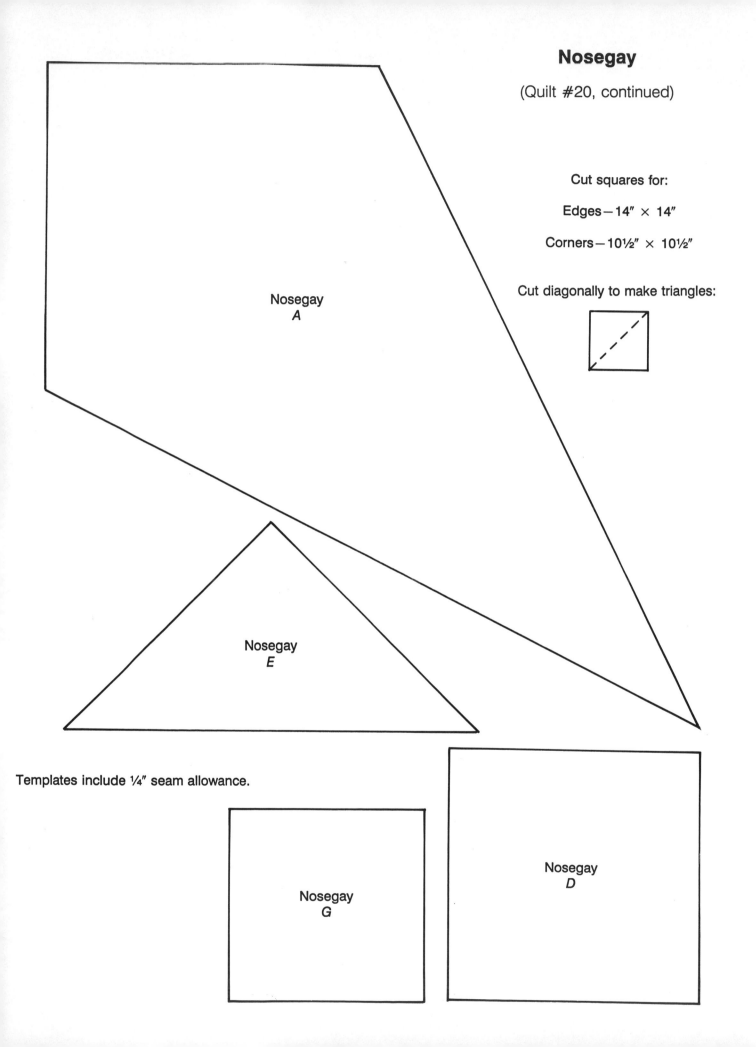

Nosegay

(Quilt #20, continued)

Cut squares for:

Edges—14″ × 14″

Corners—10½″ × 10½″

Cut diagonally to make triangles:

Nosegay
A

Nosegay
E

Templates include ¼″ seam allowance.

Nosegay
G

Nosegay
D

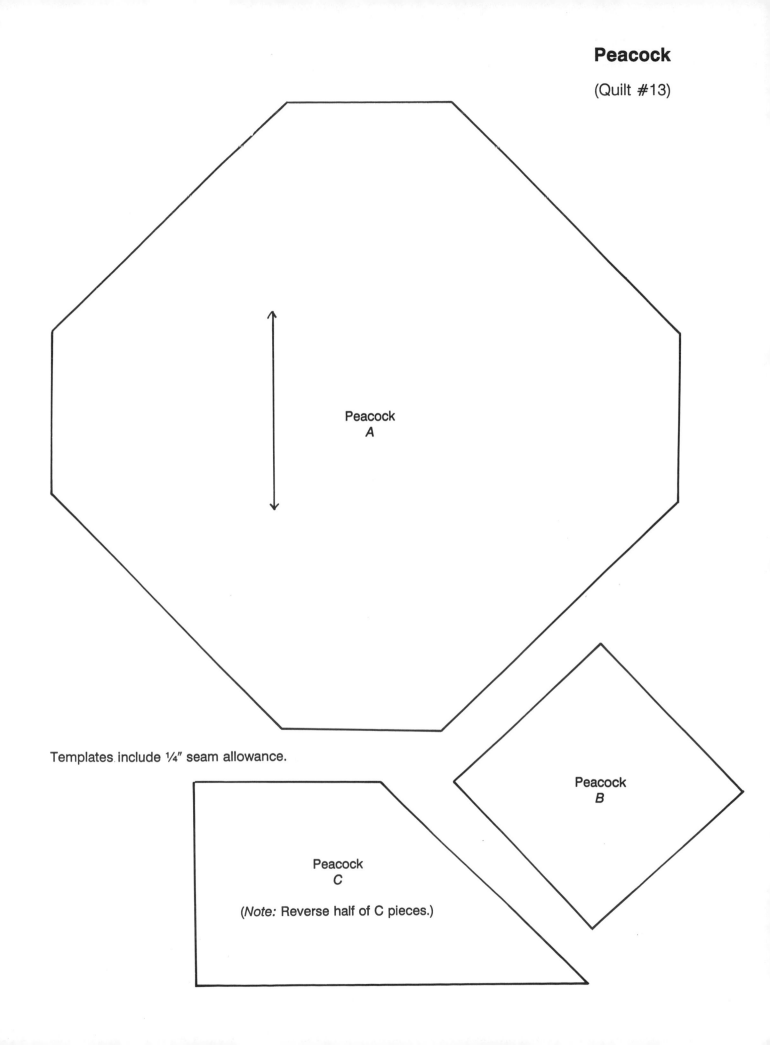

Peacock

(Quilt #13)

Peacock
A

Templates include ¼″ seam allowance.

Peacock
B

Peacock
C

(*Note:* Reverse half of C pieces.)

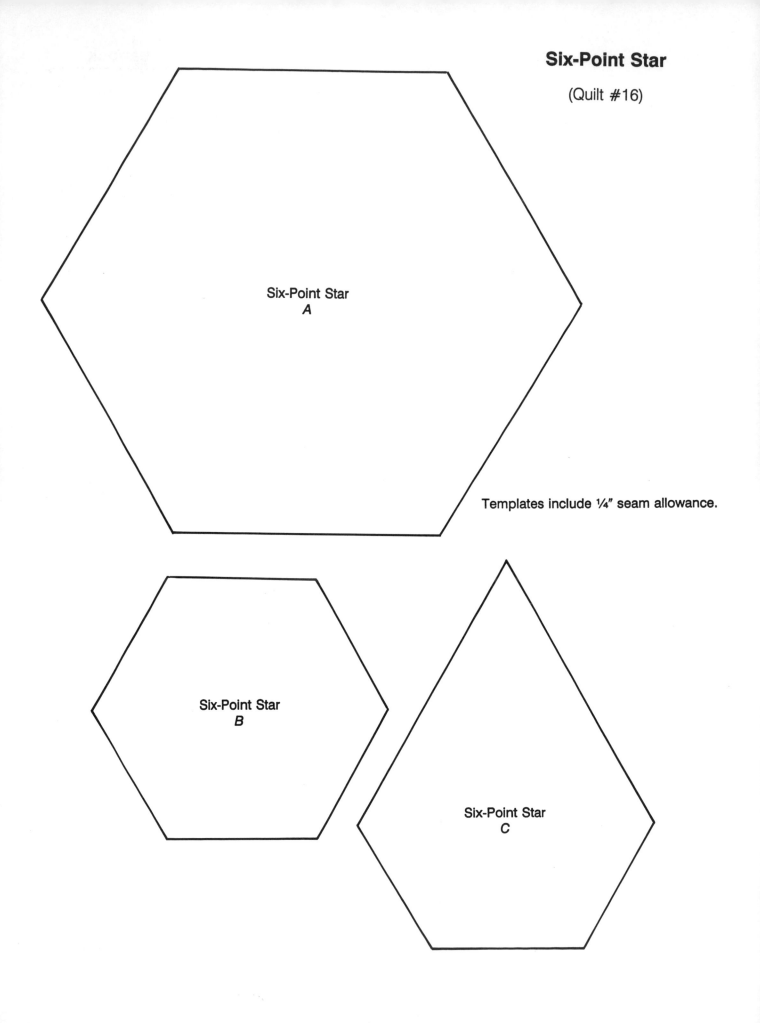

Six-Point Star

(Quilt #16)

Six-Point Star
A

Templates include ¼" seam allowance.

Six-Point Star
B

Six-Point Star
C

Texas Trellis

(Quilt #5)

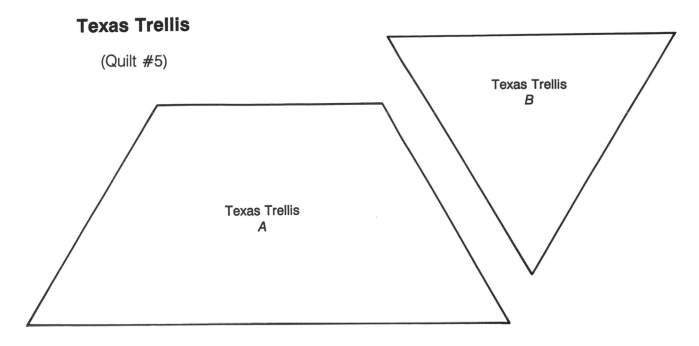

Texas Trellis
A

Texas Trellis
B

Templates include ¼" seam allowance.

Tumbling Blocks

(Quilt #7)

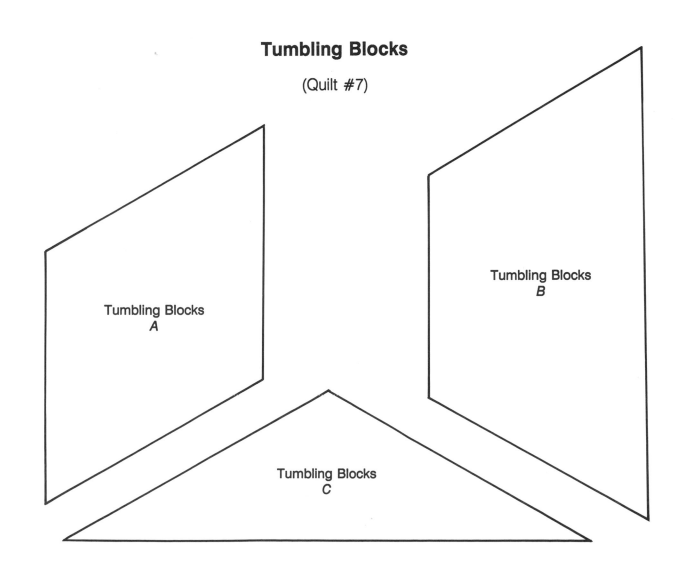

Tumbling Blocks
A

Tumbling Blocks
B

Tumbling Blocks
C

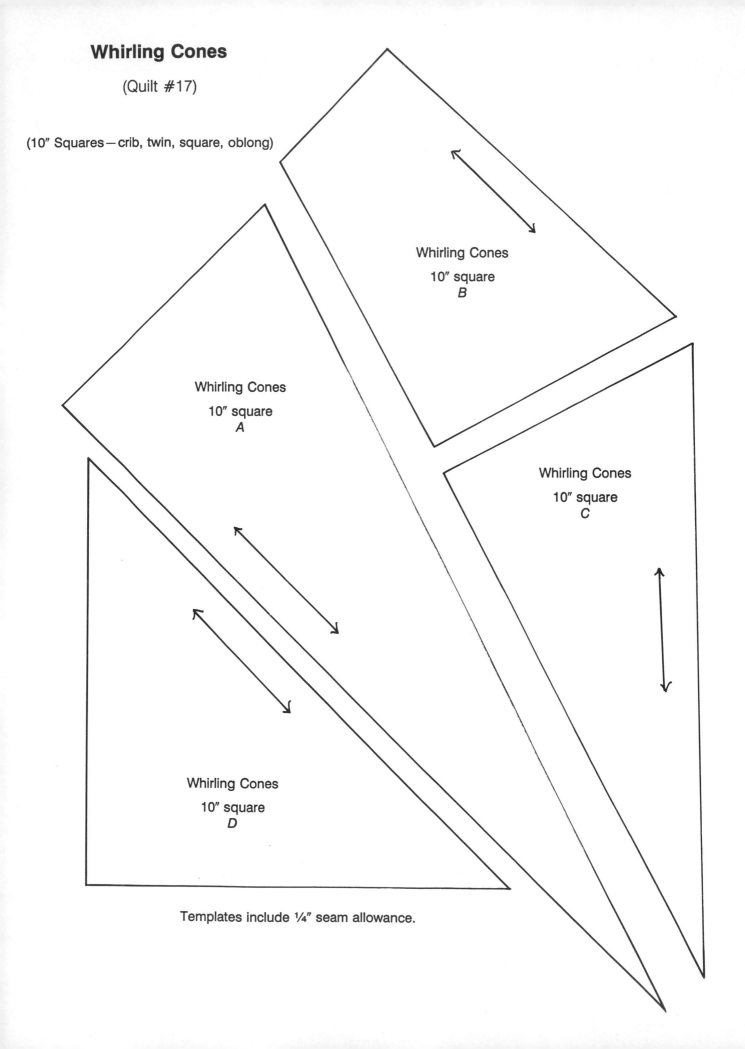

Whirling Cones

(Quilt #17)

(10″ Squares—crib, twin, square, oblong)

Whirling Cones

10″ square
B

Whirling Cones

10″ square
A

Whirling Cones

10″ square
C

Whirling Cones

10″ square
D

Templates include ¼″ seam allowance.

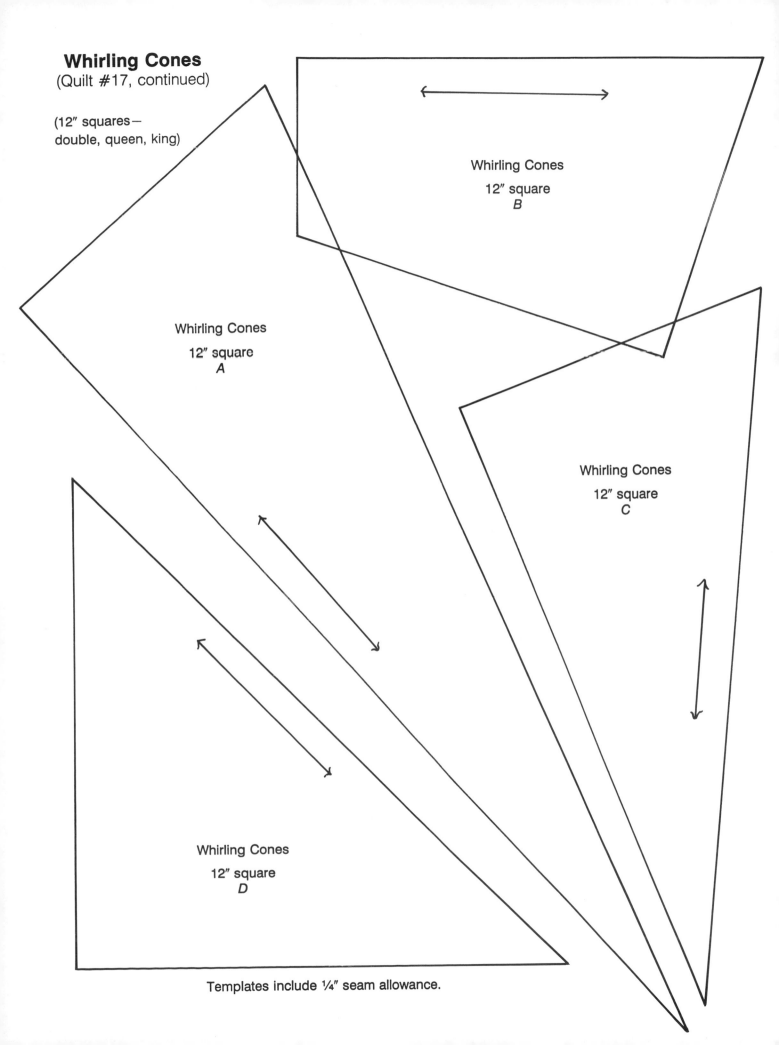

Whirling Cones
(Quilt #17, continued)

(12″ squares—
double, queen, king)

Whirling Cones

12″ square
B

Whirling Cones

12″ square
A

Whirling Cones

12″ square
C

Whirling Cones

12″ square
D

Templates include ¼″ seam allowance.

PLAY-PLAN

QUILT NAME _____ SIZE _____

TEMPLATES:

	CUT SIZE OF LATTICE STRIPS	
CUT SIZE OF LATTICE BLOCKS	
CUT SIZE OF BACK-GROUND BLOCKS	
CUT SIZE OF TRIANGLES (SIDES)	
CUT SIZE OF TRIANGLES (CORNERS)	

DARK → LIGHT

SWATCHES	PIECE A / 12	NUMBER NEEDED	LATTICE No. STRIPS / No. BLKS	BLOCKS NEEDED	TRIANGLES NEEDED SIDES / 4 CORNERS	BORDERS (CUT WIDTH) 1 2 3 4	BACKING	TOTAL YARDAGE
yds →								
yds →								
yds →								
yds →								
yds →								
yds →								
yds →								
yds →								
yds →								

PLAY-PLAN

GLOSSARY

Backing: The fabric used on the underside of the quilt.

Baste: Temporarily secure three layers together so they can be handled while quilting, often done with long stitching.

Batting: The layer between the quilt top and the backing. Gives the quilt its "puffiness."

Bias: Diagonal to the grain.

Binding: Enclosing the fabric and batting of the outer border to create a finished edge.

Block: A quilt square made of a number of smaller pieces sewn together.

Borders: Fabric used around outer areas of quilt to highlight central area and enlarge the quilt to desired size.

Grain: The direction of either the horizontal or vertical threads of the fabric. Will be either parallel to the selvage or at a 90° angle to it.

Lattice: Narrow strips sewn between blocks, used to add color and to highlight the blocks.

Lattice blocks: Small squares connecting the lattice strips.

Layout: The arrangement of blocks, lattice, and borders that make up the quilt top.

Piecing: Stitching the small pieces of fabric together.

Pin-baste: Basting with safety pins. Holds more securely than thread basting. Machine foot will not catch in the basting thread.

Quilt center: The pieced quilt, before any borders are added.

Quilting: Stitching the three layers—quilt top, batting, and backing—together.

Selvage: The woven edge along the length of the fabric.

Stitch-in-the-ditch: Quilting done in a seam line.

Template: The pattern for each piece in a block.

SUPPLY LIST

Speed-Cutting Equipment

Please check your local quilt store for Miterite, Play-Plan, and templates. If not in stock, they are available through:

Holiday Designs
507 Meadowview Lane
Coppell, Texas 75019

Check the quilt and sewing magazines for current mail-order companies. Here are some good ones:

Cabin Fever Calicoes
P.O. Box 550106
Atlanta, GA 30355

Clotilde
P.O. Box 22312 AQ
Ft. Lauderdale, FL 33335

The Country Quilter
Bonny Dr.
Somers, NY 10589

Dicmar Trading Co.
P.O. Box 3533
Georgetown Station
Washington, DC 20007

Dover Street Booksellers
39 E. Dover St.
Easton, MD 21601

Bette Feinstein
Hard-to-Find Needlework Books
96 Roundwood Rd.
Newton, MA 02164

Keepsake Quilting
P.O. Box 1459
Meredith, NH 03253

Leman Publications
6700 West 44th St.
Wheatridge, CO 80033

Nancy's Notions
P.O. Box 683
Beaver Dam, WI 53916

Quilting Books Unlimited
1158 Prairie
Aurora, IL 60506

Treadle Art
25834 Narbonne Ave.
Lomita, CA 90717

BIBLIOGRAPHY

Beyer, Jinny. *The Quilter's Album of Blocks and Borders.* EPM Publishers, 1980.

Chijiiwa, Hideaki, *Color Harmony: A Guide to Creative Color Combinations.* Greenwood Publishing, 1987.

Cody, Pat. *Continuous Line Quilting Designs: Especially for Machine Quilting.* Chilton Book Co., 1980.

Fanning, Robbie and Tony. *The Complete Book of Machine Quilting.* Chilton Book Co., 1980.

Hargrave, Harriet. *Heirloom Machine Quilting.* C&T Publishing, 1990.

Hopkins, Mary Ellen. *Baker's Dozen Doubled.* ME Publications, 1988.

Hopkins, Mary Ellen. *It's OK If You Sit On My Quilt.* ME Publications, 1989.

Johannah, Barbara. *Continuous Curve Quilting* and *The Quick Quiltmaking Handbook.* Pride of the Forest, 1980.

Johannah, Barbara. *The Quick Quiltmaking Handbook.* Pride of the Forest, 1979.

Khin, Yvonne M. *The Collector's Dictionary of Quilt Names and Patterns.* Acropolis Books, Ltd., 1980.

Leone, Diane. *Attic Windows.* Leone Publications, 1990.

McCloskey, Marsha. *Stars and Stepping Stones.* That Patchwork Place, 1989.

McClun, Diana, and Nownes, Laura. *Quilts! Quilts!! Quilts!!!* Quilt Digest Press, 1988.

McKelvey, Susan. *Light & Shadow: Optical Illusion in Quilts.* C&T Publishing, 1989.

Michell, Marti. *Quilting for People Who Don't Have Time to Quilt.* American School of Needlework, 1988.

Poster, Donna. *Speed-Cut Quilts.* Chilton Book Co., 1989.

Poster, Donna. *Dresden I.* Holiday Designs, 1989.

Seward, Linda. *Patchwork, Quilting and Appliqué.* Prentice-Hall, 1987.

Smith, Loretta. *Pineapple Quilt.* Quilt in a Day, 1989.

Tyrrell, Judi. *Beginner's Guide to Machine Quilting.* American School of Needlework, 1990.

Wood, Kaye. *Strip Quilting Projects.* Kaye Wood Publishing, 1989.